LIFE BEGINS AT

a play by

David Muncaster

Life Begins at Seventy

characters (in order of appearance)

Dorothy – in her 70s
Betty – her friend, age similar
Waitress – in her forties
Bill – in his 70s
Tom – his friend, age similar

Synopsis of Scenes

Act 1 Scene 1 – The café, early on a Wednesday afternoon.
Act 1 Scene 2 – The pub, the same as above.
Act 1 Scene 3 – The café and pub the following Thursday.
Act 1 Scene 4 – The café, fifteen minutes later.
Act 1 Scene 5 – The café, a few days later.
Act 1 Scene 6 – The café, a Thursday afternoon several weeks later.
Act 2 Scene 1 – The café, a few months later.
Act 2 Scene 2 – The pub, a few days later.
Act 2 Scene 3 - The café and pub early evening several months later, on the eve of the wedding.
Act 2 Scene 4 – The café, the following morning.

Setting: The café should be represented on one side of the stage, the pub on the other. The setting should be kept as simple as possible. When the waitress goes to fetch tea etc, she goes off. Similarly, when the men go to be served, they leave the stage. In the two scenes where action takes place in both locations simultaneously, then both areas of the stage should remain lit throughout. When the scene takes place in only one of the locations, then the other should be in darkness. Care should be taken to distinguish between exits from the café into the street and into the kitchen.

Life Begins at Seventy

ACT I Scene 1

The Café. DOROTHY is sitting with a cup of tea in front of her, pressing buttons on her mobile phone. She is conservatively dressed and quite refined. Enter Betty, who is the same age but dressed in a more modern style.

BETTY: Hello Dorothy.

DOROTHY: Mmm?

BETTY: Hello?

DOROTHY: Oh, yes. Hello.

BETTY: Am I late?

DOROTHY: Mmm?

BETTY: Am I late?

DOROTHY: Oh. I dunno.

BETTY: Right so what are we going to do today?

DOROTHY: I don't mind.

BETTY: Shall I have a cup of tea while we decide then?

DOROTHY: If you like.

BETTY: Right then. *(BETTY summons a waitress, who appears from off stage.)* Just a cup of tea please. Unless you want something Dorothy?

DOROTHY: *(Who is still fiddling with her 'phone.)* Mmm?

BETTY: Just a cup of tea. *(The WAITRESS exits. BETTY sits,)* So, how have you been?

DOROTHY: OK. Thanks.

BETTY: Been up to much since last week?

DOROTHY: Not much.

BETTY: Right. Well, I can see that I am in for a fun afternoon. Betty, your challenge is to get Dorothy to say a sentence of more than three words.

DOROTHY: What? Sorry. It's this damned thing!

BETTY: Your 'phone?

DOROTHY: Yes.

BETTY: Have you forgotten how to work it?

DOROTHY: I've lost a message.

BETTY: What do you mean?

DOROTHY: I had a message and now it's gone.

BETTY: You deleted it?

DOROTHY: No, I didn't delete it. I didn't even read it.

BETTY: Are you sure it was a message?

DOROTHY: What?

BETTY: Did it beep?

DOROTHY: Yes.

BETTY: Well, maybe it was a reminder. Meeting the glamorous Betty at two o'clock.

DOROTHY: No, that can't be right. Glamorous? I only know one Betty and that is you.

BETTY: Ha, ha. Well, did it just beep or did the message picture come up?

DOROTHY: I got the message icon.

BETTY: Icon! Get you.

DOROTHY: There's nothing wrong with using the correct terminology.

BETTY: Well, you must have deleted it then.

DOROTHY: I didn't.

BETTY: Bet you did. Pass it here.

DOROTHY passes her the phone.

DOROTHY: It's so annoying.

BETTY: *(Pressing buttons)* There's no message.

DOROTHY: Thanks. I'm glad you came.

BETTY: Nothing at all. Here. *(She passes it back.)*

DOROTHY: So. Where's it gone?

BETTY: You must have deleted it.

DOROTHY: But I didn't.

BETTY: OK then. It was a message but not from this world. It was a sign. Yes, that's it, it was a message from God.

DOROTHY: Sorry?

BETTY: What have you been up to Dot? God wants a word.

DOROTHY: What are you talking about?

BETTY: It was a sign. Telling you to repent your sins.

The WAITRESS arrives with the tea which she places in front of BETTY. She hangs about a bit, but when it is clear that neither of the ladies is going to speak again until she leaves, she goes off with the tray. BETTY sips at her tea throughout the following.

DOROTHY: Yes, you are probably right. No reason why God shouldn't embrace modern technology after all. Thunderbolts and Lightning. Old hat. Why bother when he can just send someone a text. Rpnt ur sns. That'll be it. Hold on though. I reckon, in that case, the message must have been for you.

BETTY: *(Laughs)* Yes, more than likely. You still go don't you? On Sundays.

DOROTHY: Yes.

BETTY: I don't see why you bother.

DOROTHY: You used to go.

BETTY: Only because it was expected of you. That's how it was in them days. I never believed.

DOROTHY: Really?

BETTY: Yes. I reckon half the people there never believed. People went because everyone else did. I've got better things to do on a Sunday morning.

DOROTHY: Well, that's your prerogative.

BETTY: You mean you actually believe in God?

DOROTHY: Yes.

BETTY: Still?

DOROTHY: Yes. Why else would I go to church?

BETTY: I don't know. Habit? Maybe you just never grew out of it.

DOROTHY: Grew out of it?

BETTY: Yes.

DOROTHY: I grew out of believing in Santa Claus. I grew out of believing in the Tooth Fairy. You don't grow out of believing in God. Not if you really believe. You might be right. Maybe most of the people who used to get dressed up and go to church every Sunday only did it because it was expected of them, but for me it was always important: an honour and a privilege to be in the house of God.

BETTY: Wow!

DOROTHY: I make no apology. I love my God. He is always with me.

BETTY: What's got into you today?

DOROTHY: Well, you did ask.

BETTY: He's with you?

DOROTHY: Yes.

BETTY: My God!

DOROTHY: Yes, and mine too.

BETTY: Oh no, not mine. I'm a confirmed atheist.

DOROTHY: Fine

There is a beat.

BETTY: Aren't you going to argue?

DOROTHY: Why should I?

BETTY: Aren't you supposed to save me or something?

DOROTHY: Do you want saving?

BETTY: No.

DOROTHY: That's fine then.

BETTY: I mean. It doesn't bother you that I don't believe?

DOROTHY: Not at all. God doesn't believe in atheists.

BETTY: I didn't know you were so into it.

DOROTHY: It's important to me, but I don't go round preaching. Live and let live.

BETTY: Is that why you've been keeping it secret?

DOROTHY: I haven't.

BETTY: Well. I think it's great. I'm pleased for you. Really, I am. You are one of a dying breed.

DOROTHY: Why do you say that?

BETTY: What?

DOROTHY: Dying breed.

BETTY: Well, they're all ancient aren't they? Congregations.

DOROTHY: We get some young people at the church.

BETTY: Not many I bet. It all sounds a bit 19th century. Do you pray before you go to bed?

DOROTHY: Yes. I don't know what you are imagining. It's not all long nightdresses and going to bed with a candle you know.

BETTY: Listen, if you want to go to bed with a candle that's your affair.

DOROTHY: Very funny.

BETTY: I've just got this image of you kneeling beside your bed saying your prayers.

DOROTHY: Not with my knees. If you must know I just say a few words after I have brushed my teeth.

BETTY: Does it give you a ring of confidence?

DOROTHY: *(Laughs.)* That's good. For you.

BETTY: It's quite a revelation this. I can't believe that we see each other every week and I never knew you were so into it.

DOROTHY: Well, it's not really something people talk about.

BETTY: Are you ashamed?

DOROTHY: Of course not.

BETTY: So why the secrecy?

DOROTHY: There is no secrecy. It's never come up before, that's all.

BETTY: Well, it changes things doesn't it?

DOROTHY: Don't be ridiculous.

BETTY: How can I have a serious conversation with someone who believes we are all descended from Adam and Eve?

DOROTHY: I never said that.

BETTY: You mean you don't believe that?

DOROTHY: No.

BETTY: You can pick and choose can you?

DOROTHY: It's an allusion. You shouldn't take the bible literally.

BETTY: Shouldn't you be campaigning to have Einstein banned from schools? Do you want to give up our afternoons to stand in the square with a placard yelling at passers-by?

DOROTHY: Firstly, I don't think that there are many people, regardless of how fervently religious they may be, who would argue with the theory of relativity...

BETTY: Sorry?

DOROTHY: I think you mean Darwin, and secondly, believing in God does not make me a nutter.

BETTY: Oh no. You've always been a nutter.

DOROTHY: Thank you.

BETTY: Wait a minute. Hold it just a second. I've seen you on a Sunday. Lots of times.

DOROTHY: Yes?

BETTY: In ASDA!

DOROTHY: So?

BETTY: Shopping on a Sunday!

DOROTHY: Oh behave.

BETTY: You don't believe in that either? The Lords day and all that.

DOROTHY: Give it a rest now Betty.

BETTY: Caught you out have I?

DOROTHY: Betty! Look, I don't want to fall out. You brought the subject up, now kindly drop it.

BETTY: Why are you getting angry?

DOROTHY: Betty!

BETTY: But I don't understand. Why don't you want to talk about it? You've just revealed something to me which is, well, quite shocking really. To be honest.

DOROTHY: Why? It isn't a big deal is it? What has changed? Now, I'm happy to talk to you more about this subject if it intrigues you so much, but, right now, we need to decide what we are doing this afternoon.

BETTY: OK, OK. What time is it?

DOROTHY: Half past.

BETTY: Still time to go to the cinema then?

DOROTHY: Is that what you would like to do?

BETTY: Well, it would make a change.

DOROTHY: What's on?

BETTY: I couldn't possibly tell you. With these multiplexes there's a list as long as your arm.

DOROTHY: I don't know if I fancy it.

BETTY: You always say that.

DOROTHY: I don't.

BETTY: When did we last go to the cinema?

DOROTHY: I don't remember.

BETTY: Exactly.

DOROTHY: I like it when they show the old films.

BETTY: Most of the new films are remakes of old ones anyway.

DOROTHY: Well, I don't fancy it today, anyway.

BETTY: What then?

DOROTHY: I don't mind.

BETTY: It's no good just sitting there saying 'I don't mind.' Come up with a suggestion.

DOROTHY: I'm thinking.

BETTY: We ought to plan in advance. Before we say goodbye we have to decide what we are going to do next week. OK?

DOROTHY: Yes, all right. We can pop into the cinema and see what's on next Wednesday if you like.

BETTY: Actually, I need to speak to you about next week.

DOROTHY: Oh?

BETTY: Yes. I was wondering if we could meet on Thursday instead.

DOROTHY: Why?

BETTY: For a change.

DOROTHY: What's wrong with Wednesday?

BETTY: Nothing. I just thought you might like to meet on Thursdays that's all.

DOROTHY: Thursdays. Plural? You mean from now on?.

BETTY: Yes. Maybe.

DOROTHY: But Wednesday is pensioners' afternoon at the cinema.

BETTY: So? You never fancy it.

DOROTHY: I might do if I knew what was on.

BETTY: I'll believe it when I see it.

DOROTHY: We've always met on Wednesdays.

BETTY: I know. It's just that there are these old time dancing classes and...

DOROTHY: I'm sorry?

BETTY: I thought that...

DOROTHY: Old time dancing?

BETTY: Yes.

DOROTHY: Since when have you been interested in old time dancing?

BETTY: I'm branching out.

DOROTHY: And you say that I belong to a dying breed.

BETTY: It helps keep you fit.

DOROTHY: Says whom?

BETTY: Well...

DOROTHY: Betty?

BETTY: Er...

DOROTHY: There's something you're not telling me.

BETTY: It's just, well...

DOROTHY: Does he have a name?

BETTY: Tom.

DOROTHY: Tom?

BETTY: Yes.

DOROTHY: And Tom wants to take you old time dancing?

BETTY: Yes.

DOROTHY: I see. So where did you meet Tom?

BETTY: In ASDA. We were buying suet.

DOROTHY: And they say romance is dead.

BETTY: I couldn't reach the packet. And we got talking.

DOROTHY: I see.

BETTY: He said he likes dumplings.

DOROTHY: Hmm.

BETTY: We had a bit of a laugh about it. You know. I said 'All men do'.

DOROTHY: And then he asked you to go old time dancing with him?

BETTY: Well, after a bit, yes.

DOROTHY: I see.

BETTY: What does that mean? 'I see'.

DOROTHY: Nothing.

BETTY: Michael's been dead seven years you know.

DOROTHY: I know that.

BETTY: Am I supposed to remain faithful to his memory? Is that a religious thing?

DOROTHY: Don't be silly. It just, well, it's been quite a day for revelations hasn't it?

BETTY: I suppose so.

DOROTHY: You've never shown any great interest in finding yourself a man before.

BETTY: I haven't 'found myself a man'. We just got talking and he has asked me out, that's all.

DOROTHY: I just... I don't really see what you want a man for.

BETTY: You mean you've forgotten?

DOROTHY: Come on Betty. You're seventy two!

BETTY: Well, we're only going dancing. Anyway, I thought it might be nice. I didn't know that you were going to object.

DOROTHY: I don't object.

BETTY: No?

DOROTHY: Of course not.

BETTY: But you disapprove?

DOROTHY: No, I don't disapprove either. There's no reason why we shouldn't have men friends.

BETTY: Oh aye? We? Are you looking as well?

DOROTHY: Don't be ridiculous. And what do you mean as well? You claimed that you just happened to get talking.

BETTY: Well yes, but I won't pretend that I haven't occasionally thought it might be nice to have a man about the place again. I'm not saying that that is going to be Tom. I've only just met him, but if we did get close, well, why not?

DOROTHY: Why?

BETTY: To be honest? Company I suppose.

DOROTHY: Are you lonely?

BETTY: Occasionally.

DOROTHY: Really?

BETTY: Yes. Aren't you?

DOROTHY: No.

BETTY: Never?

DOROTHY: Not really. But you see, my Frank died over twenty years ago. I've got used to it. The thought of having a man about the place now, well, I don't know where I would put him for a start.

BETTY: Well, you always were the independent one.

DOROTHY: I didn't realise that you were lonely. You should have said.

BETTY: Oh, I'm fine most of time. Let's face it, Michael was away with his job half the time anyway, so I should be used to being on my own. And, of course now, John and his wife always invite me over for Christmas and they bring the kids to see Grandma whenever they can. It's just, every now and then, I think that it might be nice to have someone to cook for, you know what I mean.

DOROTHY: I suppose so.

BETTY: Mind, it's a bit early to be talking like this. He's invited me dancing that's all. I might not even like him.

DOROTHY: Well, I hope you do and I wish you well.

BETTY: So you don't mind meeting next Thursday instead of Wednesday.

DOROTHY: Of course not. Now, what are we going to do today, whilst there is still some of the day left.

BETTY: You choose.

DOROTHY: Well, I don't really...

BETTY: If you say you don't mind again, I'm going to thump you.

DOROTHY: OK. Let's go into the city centre then. I wouldn't mind a browse around Waterstone's.

BETTY: Waterstone's it is then. You finished your tea?

DOROTHY: Before you came in.

BETTY: Right. What are we waiting for? Let's get there before they close. Oh, have you got some change for the bus?

DOROTHY: What do you mean, have you forgotten your pass?

BETTY: No, I was just thinking; what you said before.

DOROTHY: When?

BETTY: You said God is with you, right?

DOROTHY: *(Tetchy)* Yes.

BETTY: Well, you can pay his fare. He's not with me!

DOROTHY: *(Getting up)* Tcch. Go on!

BETTY: *(Getting up)* Oh of course. He's over two thousand years old. He'll have a bus pass as well.

They exit. Blackout.

ACT 1

Scene 2

The same afternoon. A public bar. Bill is in his early seventies and is dressed in denim jeans and a colourful cardigan. He is sitting at a small table. Tom approaches with two half pints of bitter. Tom is the same age as Bill, but dressed more smartly.

TOM: It's gone up again.

BILL: No!

TOM: Tuppence a pint.

BILL: Scandalous!

TOM: He says it's the brewery.

BILL: No, I reckon it goes in his pocket. Or maybe he uses the huge profits he makes to provide us with these luxurious surrounding!

They look around with disgust.

TOM: Aye. That'll be it.

BILL: I reckon it's since he's had that water meter put in.

TOM: How come?

BILL: Well, they charge him for all the water he uses now, don't they?

TOM: Yes.

BILL: Well, the amount he puts into the beer, his costs must have rocketed.

TOM: Good one Bill.

BILL: I'll ask him when I get the next round.

TOM: Aye, you do that. And I'll pick your teeth up for you.

BILL: Ha, ha!

TOM: Are you going to get them out then?

Bill empties a box of dominoes onto the table and spreads them out. They each choose their tiles and the game is played throughout the following dialogue.

TOM: Sixes? Fives? It's me then.

BILL: I see the new library is open.

TOM: Mmm.

BILL: Have you been in?

TOM: Yes.

BILL: What do you reckon?

TOM: It's OK. Bright. Functional.

BILL: Not very welcoming is it?

TOM: Maybe that's the idea. They don't want people hanging about there all day.

BILL: Why not?

TOM: Choose your books and get out. That's what they want.

BILL: The old building was cosy though, wasn't it?

TOM: I never knew it.

BILL: Really?

TOM: They were in them portakabins when I moved up here.

BILL: Is it really that long since they closed down the library?

TOM: Well, it's at least three years.

BILL: Doesn't seem that long. I must be getting old Tom.

TOM: It happens to the best of us.

BILL: No, I wouldn't fancy spending a whole morning there, reading the papers like I used to. And the noise! Libraries are supposed to be quiet places.

TOM: Only if there are people there reading. You don't need it quiet to browse the internet.

BILL: You're right there.

TOM: Anyway. I think it's great to have the facility. I mean it's not just the library in the building, there's the gallery and the function rooms.

BILL: Sounds like you've been having a good nosy round.

TOM: No, no. I just enrolled on one of the activities that's all.

BILL: Activities?

TOM: There's something going on most days.

BILL: Is there a bar?

TOM: Well, no.

BILL: So what activity has captured your imagination then? Flower arranging? Origami?

TOM: Old time dancing. Wednesday afternoons.

BILL: You're kidding.

TOM: No.

BILL: Old time dancing? You?

TOM: Why not?

BILL: I didn't know you were into all that. You are a dark horse.

TOM: To be honest I've never been much of a dancer, but it's never too late to learn.

BILL: Don't you need a partner? Hey, don't look at me. I'm not coming with you.

TOM: I've got a partner.

BILL: Oh?

TOM: Yes.

BILL: This is turning into quite an afternoon. Do tell.

TOM: There's nothing to tell. Just a lady that I met. I hardly know her.

BILL: Yet.

TOM: We've just, kind of, bumped into each other.

BILL: And you thought, ay, ay, there's life in the old dog yet.

TOM: Well, she's on her own. I'm on my own. Nothing wrong with a bit of company.

BILL: Don't blame you Tom.

TOM: So, we'll go dancing and take it from there.

BILL: Then you whisk her off her feet?

TOM: I doubt it somehow.

BILL: This could be the start of something big. New town, new girl eh?

TOM: Well, I have been here three years. You can't really accuse me of being a fast worker.

BILL: So what happens after the dancing? Would you want to, you know, take it further, I mean is it just friendship you're after, dancing once a week, or are you after company?

TOM: Both I suppose. I do miss having a woman about the place, I don't deny it. Moving here, it wasn't just to be closer to my daughter, but also a chance to make a new start.

BILL: Well, well. You've never mentioned these amorous afflictions before.

TOM: I don't know about that. All I mean is that it would never have happened down south. I mean all my friends were friends of both of us, you know what I mean. It would seemed strange asking a woman out and having everyone compare her to Molly.

BILL: I see, so it was all a cunning plan eh?

TOM: No. I never had any plans to meet another woman. But at least here I have the opportunity. I feel freer.

BILL: I've always been free myself.

TOM: Well, you never married did you? You never conformed.

BILL: No, that's me, a rebel at heart.

The game has ended, the tiles are shuffled and a new one begins.

TOM: No, I don't regret moving here. It felt like a bit of a wrench. Leaving everything behind. But I was in a rut, a fresh start was what I needed. Oh will you listen to me, at my age!

BILL: It must be because you're in love.

TOM: Oh, get away.

BILL: Life begins at seventy! So, when are you going to tell me about this murky past you've left behind?

TOM: I don't have a murky past. Very conservative really. Maybe that's what I want to leave behind.

BILL: So when do I get to meet this young lady of yours then?

TOM: I don't know that you will. I'm only taking her dancing. It might be our first and only date.

BILL: Not likely, she hasn't got a chance, you old charmer. Where did you meet her?

TOM: ASDA.

BILL: And they say romance is dead.

TOM: We just got talking, you know.

BILL: Well you must be a fast worker after all, unless you were both doing a big monthly shop.

TOM: She'd a few heavy items and a wonky wheel on her shopping trolley, so I gave her a lift home.

BILL: Ever the gentleman.

TOM: I'm glad I've still got my licence. I don't think I could cope with buses.

BILL: So you took her home, she invited you in for coffee, one thing led to another...

TOM: Behave! I didn't even intend to ask her out to be honest. It was just a way of making conversation.

BILL: You what?

TOM: You know. A lull in the conversation, I wasn't sure what to say and then I remembered the dancing classes.

BILL: Hold on, hold on. You're saying that you have accidentally asked her on a date?

TOM: Well, in a way, yes.

BILL: We've come on a date by accident. *(Chuckles.)* So you don't want to go out with her?

TOM: I didn't say that. I was pleased when she accepted. Anyway. It's one date. It will probably come to nothing.

BILL: Does she have a name? Or didn't you bother to ask?

TOM: Betty.

BILL: Well here's to you and Betty.

BILL finishes his drink. They play on in silence for a moment then the game ends. TOM drinks up and BILL picks up the glasses to get fresh halves. Whilst he is away TOM takes out a mobile phone and starts pressing buttons. BILL returns with the drinks.

BILL: I didn't know you had one of those things.

TOM: My daughter gave it to me. 'In case of emergency'.

BILL: Can you work it?

TOM: Just about. The trouble is she keeps sending me text messages about trivial nonsense, then gets annoyed that I don't reply. I mean 'Ben's got prmtd'. What is that supposed to mean?

BILL: What?

TOM: Ben's got prmtd. P.R.M.T.D.

BILL: Who's Ben?

TOM: Her eldest. My grandson.

BILL: Is he in a job?

TOM: Yes.

BILL: Maybe he's been promoted.

TOM: Oh yes. That could be it. *(He puts the phone away.)*

BILL: Aren't you going to say congratulations?

TOM: It would take me all day to say cngrts. No, I'll leave it until I see them. *(Indicating the dominoes.)* Are we having another.

BILL: Aye, in a bit. First you can tell me all about Betty.

TOM: There's not much to tell. She lives off Pear Tree Avenue and her husband died seven years ago. That's about all I know.

BILL: Not Betty Fisher?

23

TOM: Yes, that's right. Do you know her?

BILL: Oh, well, yes. Slightly. I knew Mike. Her husband.

TOM: Small world.

BILL: Isn't it. Nice chap Mike. Shame he died so young.

TOM: Heart attack when he was sixty three she said.

BILL: Yes. Nice funeral I remember. That's all I ever seem to go to these days, funerals.

TOM: So long as it's not your own. Or mine for that matter.

BILL: Oh, I'm not planning on kicking the bucket just yet. I've got a few years left in me. It's all that clean living.

TOM: That's not what I've heard.

BILL: What do you mean? I've gone to church every Sunday for the last sixty years.

TOM: Aye, but what about Monday through to Saturday?

BILL: *(Laughs)* I don't know what you're talking about.

TOM: Well, that's what I heard. Bit of a one for the ladies.

BILL: Oh aye, been checking up on me?

TOM: No. Well. No, no.

BILL: You were going to say something.

TOM: No, nothing at all. It isn't important.

BILL: Tom!

TOM: OK. Well, when I first arrived round here there was a bit of a misunderstanding that's all.

BILL: What do you mean, misunderstanding?

TOM: Just that someone said that you were a confirmed bachelor. Well, that often insinuates that...

BILL: You thought I was bent? *(Laughs loudly.)*

TOM: I was soon put right.

BILL: I don't know Tom, maybe I've turned in my old age. Come here gorgeous!

TOM: Behave yourself. You were telling me about Mike.

BILL: Was I? He was a good lad was Mike. Or Michael as Betty will call him. Funny how people have different names for home and work.

TOM: You worked with him?

BILL: He was one of the bosses. But he was never like a boss, you know what I mean? He was always one of the lads, and that got him respect. We'd all go out of our way for him because we knew he would do the same for us.

TOM: He was popular then?

BILL: Oh yeah. But he took on too much. Always away doing deals. Newcastle one day, New York the next. That's what brought on the heart attack I reckon.

TOM: Doesn't do to lead a stressful life.

BILL: So! Betty's still around is she?

TOM: Hmm?

BILL: Not done a runner like you?

TOM: I'm sorry?

BILL: I mean, not gone to start a new life in a new place.

TOM: We talked about that actually. She said that she thought I was very brave. A new start at my time of life. She said that she had thought about it, but she likes her routine, her friends.

BILL: Oh yes, I remember now. There's this old bat she hangs around with. Doris or Dorothy or something.

TOM: Dorothy.

BILL: They've known each other since school apparently. Her husband died years ago. Mike was always complaining about her, she was at the house all the time, in each other's pockets.

TOM: Betty mentioned her. They see each other once a week. Apparently they meet up each Wednesday, so Betty was going to have to ask her to change so that she could come to the dancing classes. She wasn't looking forward to it.

BILL: I'm not surprised. She's a bit of a battle axe. *(Pause,)* I mean, that's what I've heard.

TOM: Do you think I might get stood up?

BILL: No, you'll be all right. Betty can be quite persuasive.

TOM: Really?

BILL: I mean, from what Mike had told me.

TOM: You've not met this Dorothy then?

BILL: No.

TOM: Because when Betty mentioned her I said I had this pal. Maybe we could make up a foursome.

BILL: What did she say to that?

TOM: She didn't think Dorothy would be keen.

BILL: Figures. You didn't mention me by name?

TOM: I had no reason to. I didn't know you knew her.

BILL: Yes, of course.

TOM: I'll mention you next Wednesday though. See if she remembers you.

BILL: Um, yeah OK.

TOM: Are we having a decider then?

BILL: What?

TOM: Doms.

BILL: Oh, right. Yes. Look, maybe it would be better if you didn't mention me to Betty.

TOM: Why?

BILL: Well, it would just remind her of Mike. I mean you don't want to put a damper on your first date do you?

TOM: Whatever you say. Of course, if I'm going to go on seeing her...

BILL: Yes, well. Like you say, that might not happen.

TOM: True, true. But if I do see her again I'm sure she'd love to meet you sometime. You'll be able to talk over old times when you worked with her husband.

BILL: Yes. I'm sure she'd like that.

The shuffle of the tiles commences as the lights fade.

ACT 1

Scene 3

The following Thursday. Both areas of the stage are lit. DOROTHY is sitting in the café and Bill is in the pub. BETTY enters the café.

DOROTHY: I was beginning to wonder whether you had said Thursday or Friday.

BETTY: Am I late?

DOROTHY: Only if we're using earth time. I sometimes wonder if your world goes round some other sun.

BETTY: Feeling OK Dot?

DOROTHY: Fine.

BETTY: Is this how you are on Thursdays? Is this what I've been missing?

DOROTHY: I've changed my schedules to fit in with you, the least you can do is be on time.

BETTY: I'm sorry if I'm a bit late...

DOROTHY: A bit!

BETTY: Look, if you're in a mood, I'm going. I don't need it.

DOROTHY: A simple apology is all that's needed.

BETTY: I have apologised.

DOROTHY: No you haven't.

The waitress has appeared behind BETTY.

BETTY: No? Well in that case I'm sorry Dorothy, OK?

DOROTHY: Apology accepted. I'll have a fresh brew.

BETTY: If I can raise that lazy lump of a waitress.

DOROTHY: Ahem

BETTY: It's a wonder they make a go of it here.

WAITRESS: What can I get you madam?

BETTY: *(Jumping)* Ah! Um, a pot of tea for two please.

WAITRESS: Certainly, I won't be a moment.

The WAITRESS exits. DOROTHY has been holding in her laughter, but now she lets it out.

BETTY: You could have told me!

DOROTHY: I tried.

BETTY: Do you think she heard?

DOROTHY: Oh, I would think so. Better sniff the tea before we drink it.

On the other side of the stage BILL picks up his empty glass and exits.

BETTY: *(Sitting)* We'll just have a quick drink and move on. I need to get a few bits and pieces. I could do with your advice.

DOROTHY: Oh yes?

BETTY: If you don't mind.

DOROTHY: What sort of bits and pieces?

BETTY: Oh, just a few clothes.

DOROTHY: A few clothes! I take it that your date yesterday was a success?

BETTY: It went OK.

DOROTHY: So now you need a new wardrobe. It must be serious.

BETTY: I didn't say I need a new wardrobe. I just want a couple of bits that's all.

The WAITRESS enters with the tea things. On the other side of the stage TOM enters with a half pint, and sits. The WAITRESS sets down the cups, saucers and milk jugs and removes DOROTHY's used cup and saucer. The ladies don't speak until the WAITRESS exits.

DOROTHY: So, are you going to tell me what happened?

BETTY: Of course. It was very nice.

DOROTHY: Nice?

BETTY: Yes. Tom is a real gentleman. Charming and well mannered.

At this point TOM starts picking his nose and, on hearing someone approaching, searches his pockets for a handkerchief and, finding none, carefully wipes his finger under the table.

TOM: Oh, there you are.

BILL enters.

BILL: Just been to the loo. You didn't get me one in?

TOM: I didn't know you were here, did I? Sit down, I'll get you one.

BILL sits and TOM exits.

DOROTHY: He doesn't sound like your type then. Don't you prefer the rough and ready type?

BETTY: I wouldn't describe Michael as rough and ready.

DOROTHY: I wasn't referring to Michael.

BETTY: Who then?

On the other side of the stage TOM returns with a half pint for Bill.

TOM: Here you are Bill.

DOROTHY: How many were there?

BETTY: How many were there! What's got into you today? Are you deliberately trying to wind me up?

BILL: Cheers. So how did it go then?

DOROTHY: I'm sorry, take no notice.

TOM: It was nice. She's a charming woman.

BETTY: What do you want to bring it up for?

DOROTHY: Forget I spoke.

BILL: She is that. So, you'll be seeing her again?

TOM: Oh yes. Well, dancing again definitely. And maybe one or two other things.

BILL: Nudge, nudge.

TOM: I mean like museums, art galleries.

BILL: Oh. Pretty serious then?

TOM: I don't know about serious, but we hit it off OK.

BILL: Look, Tom. If you're going to be seeing her there's something you probably should know.

BETTY: It was a long time ago Dorothy.

DOROTHY: I know.

BETTY: It was out of character.

TOM: Sounds serious.

BILL: Well, it was at the time. It's just that, many years ago, Betty and I... Well, we...

TOM: You and Betty!

BETTY: I was lonely.

BILL: She was lonely. Mike was always away.

BETTY: Michael was always away.

DOROTHY: You know my feelings on the subject.

BETTY: Yes, but you never really understood did you?

TOM: What! You! Why didn't you mention this the other day?

BILL: It was a long time ago, Tom. A very long time ago.

TOM: So that's why you didn't want me to mention you to her.

BILL: I thought that if it was just one date, there was no point.

DOROTHY: I understand what being married means, Betty.

BETTY: And, of course, you've never so much as looked at another man?

DOROTHY: I haven't.

BETTY: Well, bully for you.

TOM: What do you think her reaction will be when I tell her that you're my pal?

BILL: I don't know. I haven't seen her since the funeral and that was the first time in about ten years. I've no idea what she thinks about the whole thing now.

BETTY: Oh, you don't know what you missed Dorothy. A bit of infidelity adds a bit of spice to life you know.

DOROTHY: Betty, stop it.

BETTY: OK, here's the truth. Do you want to hear it? I don't regret seeing Bill. I had a whale of a time.

DOROTHY: I don't want to know.

BETTY: Really? Don't you want to know what he was like between the sheets? He was fantastic.

DOROTHY: I'm leaving.

BETTY: He was built like a racehorse.

DOROTHY: Goodbye Betty. I'll see you when you stop behaving like an idiot.

BETTY: No you're not going anywhere. You brought this subject up. You can damn well hear me out.

TOM: Oh dear.

BETTY: God knows what Michael was getting up to on all those business trips and, frankly, I don't care. I know he wasn't the squeaky clean business man he pretended to be anyway. Why should I play the good little housewife?

DOROTHY: I can't believe I'm hearing this. You mean there were others?

BETTY: No. No, there was only Bill, and it didn't even last all that long, but it was a fantastic feeling.

DOROTHY: But, how do you know that Michael was being unfaithful? Did you have evidence? Did he tell you?

BETTY: No. But I knew. Of course he never admitted it but I knew. And there he was jetting round the world enjoying himself leaving me at home. What did he expect?

DOROTHY: I think he had the right to expect you to be waiting for him.

BETTY: Yes, well, that's your opinion. You've made your position very clear.

DOROTHY: But why Bill? I mean of all people.

BETTY: Why not?

DOROTHY: Surely you had more taste. You must have known that you were just another conquest to him.

BETTY: You don't know Bill.

DOROTHY: And he worked with Michael. Didn't that mean anything?

BETTY: Bill had no ties. He was uncomplicated.

DOROTHY: Apart from his boss being your husband.

BETTY: You never met him, did you?

DOROTHY: We didn't move in the same circles.

BETTY: The people who called him a womaniser are the people who don't know him. For a brief time he made me feel special and loved, and that is why I don't regret it.

DOROTHY: All right, all right. He's a lovely man. Silly me, taking my vows so seriously. I could have been feeling special and loved with the uncomplicated Bill!

BETTY: Dorothy, you are a self satisfied, self righteous prig.

DOROTHY: What?

BETTY: I'll choose my own clothes thanks. I don't think a nun's habit would suit me. *(She walks out.)*

BILL: Does it make a difference?

TOM: It shouldn't. It's nothing to do with me what Betty did years ago. It's a bit of a shock though.

BILL: Do you want me to talk about it?

TOM: Probably best not to.

BILL: OK.

TOM: It's none of my business.

BILL: Understood.

TOM: When was it?

BILL: Oh, must be twenty five years ago.

TOM: How long did it last?

BILL: Not long. A few months that's all. I don't think Betty ever really got used to the idea.

TOM: So, she ended it?

BILL: Yes, from what I remember. It was a long time ago Tom.

TOM: It didn't mean much to you then?

BILL: Well, I didn't see us having a future together if that's what you mean. *(BILL pauses. He obviously isn't being honest.)* Like I said, she was lonely.

TOM: So you took advantage?

BILL: Hey, back off. For someone who says it's none of his business you seem to be getting pretty het up about it.

TOM: Look, I'm sorry. It just takes a bit of getting used to. I cannot imagine that sweet lady that I took dancing yesterday having an affair.

BILL: But you can imagine your sweet dominoes partner taking advantage of her?

TOM: I said I was sorry. What more do you want? Why are you being so sensitive?

BILL: Well, you seem to have made your mind up about the guilty party.

TOM: I'm not saying anyone was guilty.

BILL: *(Seethes for a moment then seems to calm himself down.)* Oh, Forget it. I'll tell you the truth. It feels like we're talking about another person here. It's so long ago.

TOM: You've still got an eye for the ladies though, don't you Bill?

BILL: An eye, maybe, I haven't got the energy to do anything about it anymore though. I guess that makes you the playboy out of us two.

TOM: I've never been called that before.

BILL: That's what people will say about us now. Tom plays the field. Bill plays the dominoes.

TOM: I wouldn't go that far. Speaking of which, we're going to have to give it a miss today.

BILL: Oh?

TOM: There's something I need to do.

BILL: I see. This will have something to do with Betty no doubt.

TOM: Well, in a way. I just said I'd drop her in town. Save her getting the bus.

BILL: I thought she was meeting that awful friend of hers today.

TOM: Well yes. The pair of them.

BILL: Good luck. You'll need it.

TOM: She can't be that bad.

BILL: Can't she? When are you off then?

TOM: Actually, I had better be going. *(He stands.)* I'm free tomorrow if...

BILL: I'll have to check my calendar, see if I can fit you in. Come on then. *(He stands.)*

TOM: *(As he leaves)* You're coming?

BILL: Well, if you're in the mood for giving lifts, you can drop me at home.

BILL watches TOM leave then slams his fist into his hand before following him out. Then, on the other side of the stage. DOROTHY exits. Blackout.

ACT 1

Scene 4

The Café, 15 minutes later. TOM enters.

WAITRESS: Hello.

TOM: Oh hello. Er. Do you have an upstairs?

WAITRESS: 'Fraid not. This is it.

TOM: Oh.

WAITRESS: Can I get you something?

TOM: Well. Yes. A cup of tea please. That would be lovely

The WAITRESS leaves. TOM takes out his mobile and dials a number. He gets no answer and hangs up. The WAITRESS returns with the tea.

TOM: Thank you. Is it always this quiet?

WAITRESS: No, not always. In fact just now it was quite noisy.

TOM: Oh?

WAITRESS: *(Sitting.)* A couple of my regulars had a bit of a fall out. Are you meeting someone?

TOM: Yes. I thought I was late. Er, these regulars of yours...

WAITRESS: Two ladies. Seemed to be arguing about a man.

TOM: Oh dear.

WAITRESS: Do you think one of the ladies might be the person you were meeting?

TOM: It could be. I hope I haven't caused any upset.

WAITRESS: I wouldn't worry about it. These two are at it like hammer and tongs most of the time anyway.

TOM: Did they leave together?

WAITRESS: No. Well, not far apart.

TOM: Well, I think I had better...

WAITRESS: You haven't touched your tea yet. There's no point in going after them. You don't know where they've gone, do you?

TOM: No well...

WAITRESS: Which lady was it you were meeting?

TOM: Ah, well, I don't think I should really...

WAITRESS: Oh don't mind me.

TOM: No, no. It's just....

WAITRESS: *(Realising she's not going to get anything out of him.)* It's OK. I'll leave you in peace. *(BILL enters. The WAITRESS stands.)* Oh. Hello stranger. *(BILL winks at her.)*

TOM: Bill?

BILL: *(Seeing TOM for the first time.)* Oh Tom! Hello.

TOM: How did you know I was here?

BILL: I didn't. I came to... Er. I just happened to call in. This is where you are meeting Betty?

TOM: Yes. Well I thought so. I think I might have missed her.

WAITRESS: Would you like something?

BILL: Er. No. I think I won't stay. I'll see you tomorrow Tom. *(To the WAITRESS,)* I'll call again. *(He exits.)*

TOM: You two know each other?

A beat.

WAITRESS: Did you want a top up?

TOM: Hm? Oh, the tea. No I...I don't think there is any point in waiting. I think I'm wasting my time. I expect I am. Just wasting my time.

Blackout.

ACT 1

Scene 5

The Café a few days later. BETTY is sitting with the inevitable cup of tea. DOROTHY enters. Although the conversation is light at first there is a tension between them.

DOROTHY: My God. You really meant it.

BETTY: What's that?

DOROTHY: When you said you wanted to make up I didn't imagine that you would do anything so remarkable as actually arriving before me!

BETTY: Oh ha, ha. Sit down, I've ordered cakes.

DOROTHY *(Sitting)* Cakes as well! We'll have to fall out more often.

The WAITRESS enters with DOROTHY's tea and a plate of cakes. She gives the ladies a half hearted smile and exits with the tray.

BETTY: Well, you'll need your energy. I still need that new outfit.

DOROTHY: Oh. Well, we'll have to get a move on if we're getting the bus.

BETTY: That's OK. We don't need to bother with the bus today.

DOROTHY: We don't. Oh No! Don't tell me. Tom is joining us.

BETTY: Only to give us a lift. He said he had some things to do in town anyway, so he'll drop us off, then pick us up to save me carrying the bags.

DOROTHY: And what if I don't want to get in a car with Tom?

BETTY: I'll eat the cakes and you'll run for the bus. Why on earth would you refuse a lift?

DOROTHY: It's just that so seem to have it all organised.

BETTY: And I didn't consult you. Well, I'm sorry, we'll put it to the vote in future, before I accept an offer that saves us time and effort. Lighten up Dot, for God's sake. Oh no! Forget I said that. I don't want to bring Him into the conversation again.

DOROTHY: I might have know it. Wanting to make up? My foot! Just wanting your own way as usual.

BETTY: I give up!

DOROTHY: I think you would be better going shopping without me.

BETTY: I think you're right.

DOROTHY: Fine. *(She stands.)* See you around.

BETTY: Dot, sit down! *(DOROTHY sits.)* What is wrong with you? Are you jealous? Is that it? Do you want me to ask Tom if he has a friend for you?

DOROTHY: Don't you dare!

BETTY: I've met a chap. We had a nice time together. He's a nice chap. He's patient and understanding. He didn't get upset that I stood him up the other day and I'm looking forward to seeing him again, but I see no reason why you should feel threatened.

DOROTHY: I don't feel threatened.

BETTY: Well, you're acting like you do. We'll still see each other Dot. My first thought when I decided to get myself a new top was to ask you to come along with me. When I left the other day I couldn't buy anything. It didn't seem right not having you there to give me your opinion.

DOROTHY: Thanks.

BETTY: Don't thank me! And stop being childish. If you could see yourself.

DOROTHY: I'm not being childish. I'm being realistic. You don't want me around, I'm only going to get in your way. Get between you and your nice, patient, understanding chap.

BETTY: Dot!

DOROTHY: It's all becoming clear now. I'm a millstone round your neck, aren't I?

41

I'm surprised Michael put up with me. It's alright, I won't get in the way for you and Tom.

BETTY: I can't believe I'm hearing this. I'm not going to beg you Dorothy but let me just tell you that this is all in your head. Yes, I'm looking forward to seeing Tom again, but I have always looked forward to seeing you and that's for the last sixty years. Sixty years Dot! How many people in this world can say that they have been friends for sixty bloody years? Now, if you want to end all that then it's up to you, but remember that it's you. It's not me and it's not Tom.

TOM: *(Entering.)* What's not me? It looks like me.

BETTY: Ah. Oh Tom. Are you early?

TOM: I don't think so. How are you?

BETTY: I'm fine thanks.

TOM: Good. And you must be Dorothy. *(He extends his hand.)*

DOROTHY: Yes, hello. *(She reluctantly shakes it.)*

TOM: Betty's told me all about you. All good of course.

BETTY: Well, are we going then?

TOM: Oh, er *(Looking at the cakes,)* yes, I suppose the sooner we go, the sooner we get there.

BETTY: Coming Dot? *(Pause.)* Dot!

DOROTHY: Yes, yes. I'm coming.

TOM: Splendid. I'll lead the way shall I? *(He picks up the cakes and wraps the paper napkin around them before popping them into his pocket.)* You two ladies sit in the back and I'll be the chauffeur, how about that?

They all exit. Blackout.

ACT 1

Scene 6

The café on a Thursday afternoon several weeks later. BETTY is sitting alone. The WAITRESS approaches.

WAITRESS: Was there anything else?

BETTY: What?

WAITRESS: Can I get you something?

BETTY: Oh I see, yes. I have made that one cup of tea last quite a while, haven't I? I cannot understand it, it's usually me who's late. She's a stickler for time keeping, is Dot.

WAITRESS: Did you want to call her? You can use the phone in the back.

BETTY: Oh, that's very kind but I'm sure she must have left home by now.

WAITRESS: How about her mobile?

BETTY: I haven't a clue what her number is. I don't even know why she has it.

WAITRESS: Well, I'm sure she'll be along in a bit. Will the gentleman be joining you again?

BETTY: Yes. Yes, he'll be along later. I do hope she arrives before Tom. I wanted to have a word. You had better get me another tea. Make it a pot for two. See if that will make her materialise.

WAITRESS: Tea for two. *(She exits, DOROTHY appears.)*

BETTY: Ah! It was the magic word.

DOROTHY: What?

BETTY: I wondered what had happened to you.

DOROTHY: I won't sit down. I don't plan to stay.

BETTY: What are you talking about? I've just ordered tea.

DOROTHY: Well, I'm sure Tom will be happy to share it with you. I've been thinking and I've decided to give you and Tom space.

BETTY: Space?

DOROTHY: Yes.

BETTY: Have you been watching daytime TV? What's 'space'?

DOROTHY: You don't want me tagging along, no matter how nice you are about it.

The WAITRESS appears with the tea.

WAITRESS: It worked then?

BETTY: Yes.

They pause whilst the WAITRESS sets the tea things then exits.

DOROTHY: What worked?

BETTY: It's not important. Look Dot, please sit down. The tea's here, you might as well drink it.

DOROTHY: *(Sitting.)* OK. But I'm not stopping. When Tom arrives, I'll leave.

BETTY: Dot, we want you to come with us, we like having you around.

DOROTHY: You can't fool me. Why would you want me getting in your way the whole time?

BETTY: You're not in the way. And Tom and I see each other all the time. Thursday is the day we see you. We look forward to it.

DOROTHY: It's very nice of you, but I don't think you're being honest.

BETTY: I am! The thing is, Tom and I were talking and we wondered if you felt a bit awkward.

DOROTHY: See! I was right. You don't want me around.

BETTY: We do want you around, and we want you to feel comfortable. That's why Tom has asked his pal to come along today.

DOROTHY: What?

BETTY: There's no need to be afraid.

DOROTHY: How dare you?

BETTY: Dot, it will be fun.

DOROTHY: I'm off!

BETTY: Dorothy no. Wait. What's the worst that can happen? He's Tom's pal, he's coming along for the ride and if you don't hit it off, fine. He won't come again.

DOROTHY: I do not wish to be set up.

BETTY: You're not being set up. Look at it this way. He's Tom's pal. We'll have more chance to be together if he's got a pal to natter to. It'll be him and Tom, me and you.

DOROTHY: How can you do this to me? After all these years surely you couldn't imagine I would go along with this? Obviously, we both knew it wasn't working. We tried but three's a crowd. We should be making that two not four!

BETTY: But give it a try. Just this once. I promise, if it's a disaster we'll go back to how we were. No, better still, I'll tell Tom not to come on Thursdays. It'll be just me and you again. If it doesn't work.

DOROTHY: Are you trying to bribe me?

BETTY: Absolutely.

DOROTHY: I can't believe you've done this.

BETTY: Just this once, please Dot.

DOROTHY: *(Calming down.)* Who needs enemies with friends like you?

BETTY: Go on Dot.

DOROTHY: Just this once, to be polite. OK? It will be a disaster but it will be you and lover boy who looks foolish.

BETTY: Great! Thanks Dot.

DOROTHY: So who is he? This pal of Tom's.

BETTY: I don't know. I don't know anything about him.

DOROTHY: I suppose it was Tom's idea.

BETTY: No. Actually, he was dead set against the idea. I can't imagine why. First time I met Tom he was saying what a nice chap his pal was, not very similar, chalk and cheese, but he was the first person to speak to Tom when he moved up here and they've been pals ever since. But when I said, 'Why don't you bring him along?', he got all nervous and said, no, he didn't think that was a good idea. It took a hell of a lot to persuade him.

DOROTHY: Maybe he doesn't exist.

BETTY: Sorry?

DOROTHY: Perhaps he's an imaginary friend. Tom'll be roaming around now trying to find someone to come along this afternoon and pretend to be his pal. When he gets here, keep asking him questions see how well he knows Tom. It'll be like Mr and Mrs.

BETTY: Oh Dot!

DOROTHY: What's his name?

BETTY: He never said.

DOROTHY: There you are then. Tom'll be scouting around looking for a Dick or a Harry.

BETTY: Oh, it's nice to have sarcy old Dot back. I've missed her.

DOROTHY: Don't worry, I'm just getting going. Look out. Here they come.

TOM and BILL enter.

BETTY: Oh my God!

DOROTHY: Steady on.

BILL: Hello Betty.

BETTY: Oh my God!

DOROTHY: Are you having some sort of a seizure?

TOM: Sorry Betty. I just couldn't find a way to tell you.

BETTY: Oh my God!

DOROTHY: I think she must have seen the light.

BETTY: You couldn't find a way to tell me!

TOM: I tried.

BETTY: NOT HARD ENOUGH. So you knew?

TOM: Yes. But I...

BETTY: And you thought you could just waltz in here with **him** and everything would be fine?

TOM: I really didn't know how to play it.

BETTY: Any way but this way. For God's sake Tom.

DOROTHY: She has got all religious all of a sudden, hasn't she?

BETTY: Shut up Dorothy. Don't you know who that is?

DOROTHY: The new Messiah I presume.

BETTY: It's Bill

DOROTHY: Bill?

BETTY: Bill!

DOROTHY: Bill?

BETTY: Bill!

DOROTHY: BILL!

BETTY: Yes.

DOROTHY: Oh my God!

BETTY: Precisely.

TOM: Is it OK if we sit down?

BETTY: You might as well.

BILL: How are you Betty?

BETTY: I was fine up until about two minutes ago.

BILL: Quite a shock eh?

BETTY: I don't think I would have been more surprised if Michael had walked in.

BILL: I really wasn't sure about coming myself, but I thought, might as well get it over with. Tom's pretty fond of you, so you're going to have to know sooner or later.

DOROTHY: Couldn't you have found a better way to do it. Look at her! I'm not surprised from what I've heard about you Bill, but Tom. I thought you had more sense.

TOM: I thought it would be all right. I mean, I knew it would be a shock, but best to get it over with.

DOROTHY: All right! Can you possibly believe that Betty would ever want to see this man again in her life? *Do you know what he did to her?*

BILL: Now steady on!

DOROTHY: Picked her up and used her and tossed her aside.

BILL: It was nothing like that. Betty, tell her.

BETTY: Dot no. She's just protecting me. How much do you know Tom?

TOM: I know that you and Bill were close, for a short while, whilst Michael was still alive. And from what Bill tells me, you decided to end it and there were no recriminations, no arguments, and, as far as Bill is aware, Michael never knew.

BETTY: The only person I told was Dorothy. And that was after Michael died. Just after the funeral actually.

There is a pause while people gather their thoughts.

BILL: Was it seeing me at the funeral that brought it back?

BETTY: I suppose. That was a shock. I suppose I should have expected you to come, but seeing you sat there after, what was it, twenty years?

BILL: Well we did bump into each other occasionally after our... er.. but the funeral must have been the first time we had seen each other for ten years or so.

BETTY: And now here you are.

The WAITRESS appears.

WAITRESS: Can I get you anything? Oh hello.

BILL: Hello Susan.

DOROTHY: You know each other?

WAITRESS: Are you here to see me or...

BILL: *(Embarrassed)* Er. No I um...

BETTY: *(Recovering)* Still the same old Bill. No, thanks, er, Susan, we are just going.

DOROTHY: You might be. I'm going nowhere.

BETTY: Oh come on Dorothy, you agreed.

DOROTHY: That was before I knew who I was agreeing to go along with.

BETTY: Look, if I'm prepared to go along with it...

BILL: No, that's OK. She doesn't have to come if she doesn't want.

TOM: But what are you going to do?

DOROTHY: I'm going to sit here and finish my tea. That's what I'm going to do. Susan! I'll have a slice of walnut cake please.

WAITRESS: OK.

The WAITRESS exits.

BETTY: Dorothy.

BILL: It's OK Betty. I understand how Dot...

DOROTHY: Dorothy!

BILL: ..Dorothy feels. You shouldn't try to force her. So, come along. It's narrow boats today, wasn't that the plan?

TOM: Well, yes.

BILL: Come on then. Before all the locks dry up.

TOM and BETTY move toward the exit. BILL doesn't move.

TOM: Aren't you coming?

BILL: No, I think I'll just stay here awhile.

BETTY: I really don't think...

BILL: I'm not very interested in narrow boats to be honest.

TOM: Bill?

BILL: Of you go then.

TOM: Bill, I really think you should...

DOROTHY: Oh get off for God's sake. I can look after myself.

BETTY: Are you sure?

DOROTHY: Go!

BETTY: OK.

BETTY and Tom exit as the WAITRESS appears with a slice of cake for DOROTHY.

BILL: Looks delicious, did you bake it yourself Susan?

WAITRESS: Of course.

BILL: You always were good in the kitchen.

The WAITRESS smiles and exits.

DOROTHY: Another one of your conquests? Bit young isn't she?

BILL: You really don't have a very high opinion of me do you.

DOROTHY: Let me put it this way. I have lumps of old cheese in my fridge that I hold in a higher esteem than you.

BILL: Mmmm.

DOROTHY: And I would probably have a better conversation with them.

BILL: Betty always said you had a razor sharp wit. Why did you take so against me?

DOROTHY: Oh, it's your brown shoes. What do you think?

BILL: It takes two to tango.

DOROTHY: Yes but it's usually the man that does the leading.

BILL: I'm going to be honest with you. Now, I'm not really one for wearing my heart on my sleeve, but Tom is my pal and he's pretty fond of Betty. You and me are going to have to sort ourselves out for their sake. You understand? We have to learn to at least be civil to each other.

DOROTHY: For the sake of their relationship? Don't make me laugh, you weren't to bothered about her relationship with Michael!

BILL: It was a very long time ago.

The conversation pauses. DOROTHY eats her cake.

BILL: OK, no excuses. You know my reputation. It's exaggerated of course, but I had no problem with being thought of as a bit of a stud.

DOROTHY snorts, splattering crumbs.

BILL: But, once I got to know her, I realised that she was a very special person. Someone to be cherished.

DOROTHY: Like all the others? *(She dabs her mouth with a handkerchief.)*

BILL: I'm not giving you a line here. It's the truth. I fell in love.

DOROTHY: *(Dubiously.)* Honestly?

BILL: As God is my judge. For the first time in my life, I wanted to settle down, but I knew that she would never leave Michael. I haven't even told her this, Dorothy, I'm trusting you here.

DOROTHY: So, supposing this is true, what did you do?

BILL: I told her that I just wanted to make her happy. I would always be there for her. In the end the guilt got too much for her and she ended it. It took me a long time to get over her Dorothy. A long time.

DOROTHY: But you managed it?

BILL: I know that you don't approve of what we did. But you've forgiven her haven't you?

DOROTHY: I suppose so.

BILL: Do you think you can try to forgive me?

DOROTHY: Why?

BILL: Because if we can get along it will be nicer for Tom and Betty.

DOROTHY: You said you loved her.

BILL: Yes.

DOROTHY: So what about now. How do you feel now? You've missed out again, haven't you?

BILL: What do you mean?

DOROTHY: Wouldn't you rather be in Tom's shoes?

BILL: No. It would never work. Me and Betty? Too much history.

DOROTHY: So you're happy for her to go waltzing off into the sunset with your best pal?

BILL: If it makes her happy.

DOROTHY: How very magnanimous.

BILL: That's me always puts others first. *(He notices DOROTHY has finished her cake.)* Come on then.

DOROTHY: What?

BILL: Let's get going.

DOROTHY: Look, I do see your point and I am prepared to tolerate you for Betty's sake but I am not, repeat not, leaving this café with you.

BILL: Why not?

DOROTHY: This reputation of yours that you are so proud of. I have no intention of being seen as another one of your conquests.

BILL: Dot...

DOROTHY: Dorothy!

BILL: Dorothy, I'm seventy three!

DOROTHY: I don't care how old you are.

BILL: There's hardly anyone left alive who remembers me as a young man. Now I'm just Bill from St Mary's'.

DOROTHY: Oh, that was a bit clumsy.

BILL: What?

DOROTHY: I suppose you've heard that I go to church, so you thought you would drop that line in order to make me think we'd got something in common.

BILL: I didn't know you went to church. At least I know you don't go St Mary's.

DOROTHY: No. All Saints.

BILL: There you are then. I think I might have seen you if you did go to St Mary's, at some point in the last sixty years.

DOROTHY: Sixty years!

BILL: Man and boy.

DOROTHY: And how does sleeping with half the women in the area square with your religious views?

BILL: I take that as an insult. Only half!

DOROTHY: This is not a joking matter.

BILL: It's a complicated subject. Now I'm quite happy to sit here and have theological discussion if that's what you want, but I rather thought we would pop along to the multiplex and see The Sound of Music.

DOROTHY: I'm sorry?

BILL: It starts at three fifteen. We have plenty of time if we leave now.

DOROTHY: The Sound of Music?

BILL: Yes.

DOROTHY: Why on earth are they showing The Sound of Music?

BILL: I wouldn't know.

DOROTHY: Is it a re-make?

BILL: No it's the original. They show old films on Thursday afternoons now.

DOROTHY: I thought Wednesday was pensioners' day.

BILL: I don't know about that. What I do know is that the Sound of Music is on this afternoon. Now, do you fancy it or not?

DOROTHY: I don't know.

BILL: Don't you like Julie Andrews?

DOROTHY: We've nothing in common Bill. What's the point?

BILL: You and Julie Andrews?

DOROTHY: You and me. You know that's what I meant.

BILL: We have got something in common. We both like Julie Andrews.

DOROTHY: I didn't say I like her. I don't dislike her.

BILL: OK, we both don't dislike Julie Andrews then. Come on Dot.

DOROTHY: Dorothy!

BILL: Dot!

DOROTHY: Dorothy!

BILL: Dot!

DOROTHY: William!

BILL: William? Nobody has ever called me William. OK, William then. Come on. The nuns are waiting.

CURTAIN

ACT 2

Scene 1

The café, several weeks later. The waitress is sitting at the table reading a magazine. DOROTHY and BILL enter. She hides the magazine behind her back and smiles.

BILL: Hello there. A pot of tea and four straws please.

WAITRESS: Certainly. Anything else?

BILL: A crocodile sandwich and make it snappy!

DOROTHY: Nothing thank you.

WAITRESS: Thank you.

The WAITRESS exits.

BILL: Well, I wonder what delights are in store for us today. An exhibition of bus tickets? A foreign language film about goats in Afghanistan? A trip to the Dulux factory to watch paint dry?

DOROTHY: Bill, don't be rotten.

BILL: I hope it's the Dulux factory.

DOROTHY: Anyway, we may not go anywhere today, after what we have to say.

BILL: True. That'll be a disappointment for Tom. I'm sure he does it to annoy us.

DOROTHY: Anyone would think that you don't enjoy our days out together.

BILL: I always enjoy my days out with you Dot. Not as much as the days in...

DOROTHY: Bill, behave yourself!

BILL: It's Tom. I never realised he was such a boring b...

DOROTHY: Bill!

BILL: Sorry. You have to admit it though.

DOROTHY: His tastes are, well, a little conservative I suppose.

BILL: I can't see what Betty sees in him. As a dominoes partner he was fine. You don't expect sparkling conversation when you're playing doms, but...

DOROTHY: Is he very different from Michael?

BILL: Well, you knew Michael.

DOROTHY: Not really. I tended to stay away when he was at home. I got the impression he didn't like me very much.

BILL: I wonder why.

DOROTHY: Hey. Watch it, I might change my mind. You're skating on thin ice yourself!

BILL: I'd better go on a diet then.

DOROTHY: A diet?

BILL: So I don't fall through.

The WAITRESS brings the tea things, sets them and exits.

DOROTHY: He must have had something about him though. He rose up pretty high in the firm.

BILL: He was a great bloke. Everyone's pal. I never met anyone who didn't like him. Gregarious, he was.

DOROTHY: Not quite like Tom then?

BILL: He's not in the same league. You didn't cross him though. Get on the wrong side of him and he would never forgive you.

DOROTHY: Did you get on the wrong side of him? *(Pause.)* Bill ?

BILL: Are you sure you want to talk about this?

DOROTHY: It's probably better to get it out in the open.

BILL: They'll be here any minute.

DOROTHY: I've never known Betty be anything less than ten minutes late. We've plenty of time.

BILL: OK. But warn me if you see them. I don't want Betty walking in when I'm mid sentence.

DOROTHY: Deal.

BILL: I don't really know where to begin.

DOROTHY: I'll start you then. Please don't be offended, I'm just being honest. If you thought so much of Michael how could you possibly enter into an affair with his wife?

BILL: The thing is... He was a great guy. One of the lads, he didn't seem like a boss, more like a mate. But he was ruthless. That's why he got on in the company. You stayed on his good side if you knew what was good for you. We worked for him and he got the best out of us by being our pal, but I saw the way he treated other people. If he didn't need you, then you were just nothing to him. A guy I worked with for a while, Charlie, went to join another team. Before he left Mike was great with him, treated him like a brother, just like he did the rest of us. As soon as he left, he dropped him. It was like he never existed. The only time he did acknowledge his existence was to put him down.

DOROTHY: Well, I think a lot of people in business are like that.

BILL: No, Mike went one stage further. If you crossed him, he treated you like dirt.

DOROTHY: OK, so he wasn't the perfect man he seemed, but I still don't see what this has to do with you and Betty.

BILL: She'll never say a word against him but, believe me, he made her life a living hell.

DOROTHY: I don't believe you.

BILL: I'm the only person she has ever told. It's true. He was so cruel to her.

DOROTHY: I would have known.

BILL: You'd think so, I know you were close, but Betty is very good at keeping things to herself, even from her friends. But he really hurt her.

DOROTHY: How?

BILL: Mental cruelty. Ignoring her. Calling her names. One time she cooked a lavish meal, he dumped it in the bin and got himself a takeaway, all because she asked him not to salt it before he had tasted it.

DOROTHY: She told you this?

BILL: She couldn't understand why he had changed, what she had done to him.

DOROTHY: What had she done to him?

BILL: Nothing. She put up with years of mistreatment. Mistreatment that she never deserved.

DOROTHY: Well, I certainly can't imagine her deserving mistreatment.

BILL: If you ask me it was guilt. I've seen a lot of that, guilt. Betty never did anything wrong, but he did something to make *him* feel guilty. I've no proof, but it will be some woman in some town, of that I'm sure. And guilt made him treat Betty like it was her who had done him wrong.

DOROTHY: This is incredible.

BILL: The things you don't know eh?

DOROTHY: So, why did she tell you? How did you and Betty get together?

BILL: Pure accident. I gave Mike a lift to the airport when he was off on one of his business trips. When we got his bags out of my boot, it seems that I had picked up a bag that wasn't his, so I took it back. When I got to the house, Betty opened the door trying to cover her face. I thought he had hit her and made her move her hand, but she had just been crying. He had been yelling and shouting at her before he left, but she's put on a show when I was there. Soon as we left she had broken down and was still crying when I returned an hour later. I made her tell me all about it and I suppose I became her support for a while.

DOROTHY: And you began an affair.

BILL: That wasn't my intention, I promise you. But she had bottled everything up for so long, it all just came pouring out and we became close. I think I was something of a lifeline for her. Don't be hurt, she couldn't tell you because you went back so far.

DOROTHY: So why did she end it? Did she end it?

BILL: Yes. I don't know. Maybe simple fear that we would get caught?

DOROTHY: Do you think so?

BILL: Not really. Guilt probably. There it is again. Guilt. I tried to get her to leave him. This will come as a shock to you, but I would have married her. She only had to say the word.

DOROTHY: But she wouldn't.

BILL: She's stubborn, is Betty. She kept saying it was for better or worse. Funny thing about her. Now she is in her seventies, she seems to have a more modern outlook on life than she did in her forties!

DOROTHY: Well, we all adapt to modern life, don't we?

BILL: Are you including yourself in that statement?

DOROTHY: Of course!

BILL: Some people would see you as very traditional.

DOROTHY: The fact that I am allowing myself to be courted by you is a big step for me, I can tell you. I can hardly believe it myself.

BILL: Is that what I'm doing? Courting you?

DOROTHY: What would you call it?

BILL: I don't know. Courting implies romance.

DOROTHY: Does it?

BILL: I'd say so.

DOROTHY: Well, we had better think of another word then.

BILL: No. I like courting. I feel quite privileged.

DOROTHY: So you should. You are only the second man to do so.

BILL: Really. Frank was your first?

DOROTHY: Childhood sweethearts we were.

BILL: Well, I will try to honour his memory.

DOROTHY: I'll make sure you do.

BILL: It must have been difficult for you. When he died.

DOROTHY: Well, seeing as we are being honest with each other, yes it was. I had built my life around Frank. When he died I didn't know what to do with myself. That's when I started seeing a lot of Betty. My God, I never realised what she was going through herself! I never had an inkling.

BILL: She's a remarkable woman.

DOROTHY: You're still fond of her.

BILL: Of course. I never forgot her. I put it to the back of my mind. After all, life has to go on but yes, I am still fond of her. But I don't want to step into Tom's shoes if that's what you're thinking.

DOROTHY: I don't think either Tom or Betty would let you anywhere near his shoes. Bill, are you sure we are doing the right thing? I mean, it's a difficult thing to undo if it doesn't work.

BILL: Positive. And it's you that wants to formalise it.

DOROTHY: Yes, but even so...

BILL: Neither of us are getting any younger Dot. I may not have been a good man but I have always tried to make people happy, and that's what I intend with you.

DOROTHY: Well, thank you. I hope we continue to enjoy each other's company. It will make life a lot easier.

BILL: And if not, we'll be miserable but rich!

DOROTHY: Not exactly deep are you Bill ?

BILL: No, but my shallowness is quite profound!

TOM and BETTY enter.

BETTY: Who's shallow?

BILL: Hoosh hello Betty. Hoosh hello Tom.

BETTY: Always the joker. Got enough tea have you?

BILL: I ordered enough for you pair several hours ago, when we were supposed to be meeting.

BETTY: Sorry. My fault.

TOM: Not at all. I think I was a little late picking you up.

BETTY: Isn't he a gentleman? So, are we going, make up for lost time.

DOROTHY: Bill and I have something to say first. Did you want some tea?

The WAITRESS is hovering.

BETTY: Sounds serious. I think we had better.

BILL: We had better have a fresh pot.

The WAITRESS takes the pot and exits.

BETTY: So what have you got to tell us? Oh don't say you've fallen out. I'm just starting to enjoy our little trips.

DOROTHY: No, we haven't fallen out.

BETTY: Good.

DOROTHY: We've decided to get married.

Long Silence.

BETTY: I'm sorry. Ha! For a moment there I thought you said that you had decided to get married.

DOROTHY: That is correct.

BETTY: Have you gone completely mad?

DOROTHY: Probably.

TOM: Congratulations old man.

BILL: Thank you.

BETTY: But why?

DOROTHY: Contrary to expectations, we enjoy each other's company and, actually, have been seeing quite a lot of each other recently. Bill has been coming over most days...

BETTY: Really?

DOROTHY: ...and going home after dinner, but we thought that there is no point in keeping two houses when we can live in one. My house is plenty big enough for both of us and the money Bill gets from the sale of his will give us a very necessary financial boost.

BETTY: But, married!

DOROTHY: You don't expect me to 'bunk up' with someone?

BETTY: So, let me get this straight, this is a financial arrangement. You haven't fallen madly in love.

DOROTHY: We er...

BILL: We enjoy each others company and Dot's house is big enough so that we won't get under each others feet.

The WAITRESS arrives with the tea giving BILL a knowing look before she exits. BILL looks a bit sheepish.

BETTY: *(Who has noticed BILL and the WAITRESS.)* Dorothy. Um, can we just go somewhere for a chat?

DOROTHY: Why?

BETTY: It's such a shock, I think we should...

DOROTHY: Thank you Betty but I have thought this through quite thoroughly. A lot of women my age are in homes, old peoples homes I mean, where they share their residence with men they hardly know. Over the last couple of months I have grown to realise that I can tolerate Bill...

BILL: Thanks.

DOROTHY: ...in fact, I quite enjoy his company. That being the case, I have no objection to him occupying an adjacent room to my own. You can think of it as Bill and I moving into a home, except that it happens to be the home where I currently reside.

BETTY: But you're getting married?

DOROTHY: Of course. As my house isn't actually an old people home our marriage is necessary to avoid unnecessary scandal.

BETTY: Scandal!

DOROTHY: God will understand, but I can't say the same for the neighbours.

BETTY: Well, this is a cause for celebration, I think. I'm not really sure to be honest.

TOM: Of course it is. Congratulations Bill, Dorothy, I'm sure you'll be very happy.

BETTY: Did you hear what she just said?

TOM: A wedding is a wedding. Best wishes to you both.

DOROTHY: Thank you.

BILL: Cheers Tom.

TOM: I'll tell you what. Let's clear out of here. Let's do something wild to celebrate.

BILL: I can hardly wait.

DOROTHY: What about the tea?

TOM: Tea? How can you celebrate with tea? Champagne is what we need.

BILL: But it's here.

TOM: *(Beckoning the WAITRESS.)* I'm sorry, there's been a change of plan. *(He hands her a twenty pound note.)* Sorry for any inconvenience.

WAITRESS: Oh. Well, I'll get your change.

TOM: Keep it. This is a special day. Come on then you three, follow me!

The three follow TOM out slightly aghast at his behaviour. Blackout.

ACT 2

Scene 2

The pub a few days later. Bill is sitting nursing his half pint. Betty enters.

BILL: Betty! You came.

BETTY: I'm not sure this is a good idea. Couldn't we have met in the café? What if Tom comes in?

BILL: He won't. What are you having?

BETTY: Oh, gin and tonic.

BILL exits to get the drink. BETTY takes out her lipstick and a mirror and starts to apply the make-up.

BILL: *(Off.)* Do you want ice?

BETTY: In this weather?

She completes her make-up and puts the stuff away. Bill returns with the drink.

BILL: There you are. You wouldn't get that in the café.

BETTY: True enough. So, what's all this about?

BILL: I just thought it a good idea for us to have a chat, you know, before the wedding. It must have come as a shock to you.

BETTY: I couldn't have been more surprised.

BILL: Sorry Betty.

BETTY: No need to apologise, but it seems like a pretty weird arrangement if you ask me.

BILL: She's a very practical woman, is Dorothy. I need to be honest with you Betty. I've grown pretty fond of her actually. I'm looking forward to spending my remaining days with her. You and me, well it was a long time ago.

BETTY: You and me? Bill, if you think that you're breaking my heart my marrying my best friend, you are very much mistaken.

BILL: That's good to hear.

BETTY: I think you're barking mad, but that's your affair.

BILL: That's great.

BETTY: I would never have believed it. Dot! After all these years. And with you!

No offence but you're not much like Frank.

BILL: No, well. I don't think anyone could replace Frank.

BETTY: Yes, you're probably right. Maybe the reason that she likes you is because you are so different from Frank.

BILL: Yes, that could be it.

BETTY: So, what did you want to see me about.

BILL: Um, well. That's all really.

BETTY: That's all? You've had me catch two buses to get here just to discuss the fact that you're not much like Frank?

BILL: No, I mean I wanted to make sure that you are OK with it.

BETTY: OK with what?

BILL: Well, with me marrying Dorothy of course.

BETTY: Why shouldn't I be? She's old enough to know what she's doing.

BILL: And you really don't mind?

BETTY: Mind?

BILL: You're not too upset?

BETTY: Upset? What is this Bill? Am I supposed to be devastated that you're marrying Dorothy?

BILL: Well, I...

BETTY: I don't believe it. Older but no wiser eh?

BILL: I don't...

BETTY: I'm sorry Bill but there is obviously some misunderstanding here. Listen, I have something to tell you that is obviously going to come as something of a shock. More of a shock than Dorothy telling me that the pair of you have decided to get married. I haven't been entirely straight with you Bill. I thought you knew.

BILL: Knew what?

BETTY: You mean that you never suspected?

BILL: I really don't know what you are talking about.

BETTY: But. Surely you must have... OK, let's go back 25 years and start at the beginning. In fact, let's go right back to the beginning, before I even knew you. Michael was a bastard. You know that. He treated me like dirt. But he always had, Bill. We had been married twenty years before I met you and nothing had changed since the first day of our marriage. I nearly walked out on him a number of times, but there was one thing that stopped me every time. Money. Not very liberated of me I know, but Michael earned a good wage and it kept me in the manner to which I had become accustomed. That and the bonuses, if you know what I mean.

BILL: Bonuses?

BETTY: The little extras that the tax man never got to hear about.

BILL: Mike was on the take!

BETTY: Naturally. Oh don't look so shocked! Everyone was in those days. Well, everyone who had the opportunity anyway. So, I put up with the way he treated me because along with *him* came a lifestyle that I rather enjoyed. He was away a great deal of the time anyway and I found a way to cope with him when he was at home. When he was away, I acted like I was a rich widow, and when he was home, I just pretended to be everything that he wanted me to be. I told him that it would be silly of me to get upset because he was in a bad temper because he had a very stressful job and it was my duty to help him relax when he got home. He liked that. But all the time I was controlling him because he never saw the real me. Weeping and begging wouldn't have achieved anything but smiling and appearing to be a 'good little housewife' made me stronger.

BILL: You put on an act?

BETTY: Yes, and it put me in control.

BILL: I'm not convinced.

BETTY: But it's true Bill. He even started treating me better. Once he realised that I wasn't going to break down in tears every time he raised his voice he didn't bother any more. But there was just one thing missing. I knew he was carrying on when he was away. I saw his receipts, his credit card statements. He was playing away from home, and that made me angry. It was the one thing that he did that still got to me, and I wanted revenge. I wanted some of the same, but how could I have an affair without him getting to hear about it? Simple, I involve myself with the biggest playboy in town! Someone who knew how to be discreet. Someone who was well practiced at extra marital affairs. Someone who wouldn't get emotionally involved. The fact that he happened to work for my husband made it even better.

BILL: Now I know you are not serious.

BETTY: I'm telling you the truth Bill.

BILL: I don't believe it.

BETTY: Remember the extra bag in the car that day you took him to the airport? I put it there because I knew you would bring it back. I spent an hour rubbing my eyes to make them red. 'Oh Bill, he's so beastly to me' - does that sound familiar?

BILL: Why are you doing this?

BETTY: We both played are our characters brilliantly. I was the poor abused housewife, tortured by a loveless marriage; you were the knight in shining armour bringing me a bit of joy into my miserable existence.

BILL: Betty, stop it now.

BETTY: Don't you like what you are hearing Bill?

BILL: You're making yourself look ridiculous.

BETTY: Why ridiculous?

BILL: If all this is then why did you end it?

BETTY: Because you fell for me Bill. Mr Love-them-and-leave-them went and fell in love with me. I had to end it before it got complicated.

BILL: Very good Betty. An excellent story. Look! I know I've hurt you and I'm sorry, but you have Tom, he's a good man. He'll make you happier than I ever would have done.

BETTY: Bill, I'm not making all this up. OK, I've simplified things a little, but I'm telling you the truth. I thought you had already realised it yourself.

BILL: Yes Betty.

BETTY: Oh, it doesn't matter if you don't believe me. It's out in the open, what you make of it is up to you. And yes, Tom is a good man. A gentleman. Everything that Michael wasn't.

BILL: I do still care for you Betty.

BETTY: I know you do Bill. And I've been callous. I don't know, somehow I thought we both knew that we were only playing a game. I'm sorry. I didn't realise that you hadn't worked it out. I hope you will forgive me, and I wish you and Dorothy all the best.

BILL: Thank you.

BETTY: And you make sure that you treat her right. She's my best friend, remember.

BILL: I will, don't worry about that.

BETTY: No more womanising.

BILL: I stopped all that after… I mean, a long time ago.

BETTY: Yes Bill, sure you did. That's why you didn't want to meet me in the café.

BILL: Sorry?

BETTY: Bit close for comfort was it?

BILL: Oh, I think you've got that wrong...

BETTY: Just remember, you've been warned.

BILL: Yes. OK, Betty.

BETTY: Anyway. I'd better be getting back. And you must have plenty to do as well. Aren't you getting married soon?

Blackout.

ACT 2

Scene 3

It is the eve of the Wedding. Both areas of the stage are lit. TOM and BILL enter the pub.

TOM: Right. You sit yourself down and I'll get the drinks.

BILL: Fair enough.

TOM exits. BETTY and DOROTHY arrive in the cafe. The WAITRESS appears.

BETTY: I don't know why we have come in here, they must be about to close.

WAITRESS: You're OK for a while yet.

DOROTHY: I am not going into a public house Betty. I have never been into one and I do not intend to start now.

BETTY: *(Sighs)* Two teas please.

WAITRESS: Righto.

The WAITRESS exits. TOM returns to BILL with two pints.

BILL: That's how you can tell it's my stag night. I'm drinking pints!

TOM: And you won't need your wallet tonight Bill.

BILL: Why. Are we only having the one?

TOM: You know what I mean. Are you sure you are happy to be here? We can go somewhere else. How about a pub crawl?

BILL: No, I'm happy here Tom. And I don't think you've been on a pub crawl in your life.

TOM: Maybe. Anyway, cheers!

BILL: Cheers!

They drink.

TOM: Who would have imagined it eh?

BILL: Not me anyway. I didn't imagine I would ever get wed. She's a persuasive woman is Dorothy.

TOM: I wonder how much persuading you needed.

TOM is gulping his drink down.

BILL: Are you thirsty?

TOM: Got to make the most of it. I can't see me going to many more stag dos.

BILL: It's hardly a stag do, is it Tom? You and me in our local. We only need to get the doms out and it's the same as any other night.

TOM: Doesn't matter. It's your wedding tomorrow and we're getting drunk!

TOM finishes his pint. With a shake of his head BILL also drains his glass and TOM exits to get refills. In the café, the WAITRESS returns with the tea which she sets.

WAITRESS: Anything else?

BETTY: No that's fine. Oh, sorry Dorothy, did you want anything?

DOROTHY: No thanks.

WAITRESS: I'll leave you in peace in.

The WAITRESS exits. The women look at each other, seemingly unable to think of anything to say.

BETTY: Oh this is ridiculous. Sitting in a cafe that's about to close, on your hen night!

DOROTHY: I would be grateful if you didn't use that term. Hen night indeed.

BETTY: Well call it what you like, I'm not staying here.

DOROTHY: Fine. I'm happy to go home, it was your idea to come out.

BETTY: How about a hotel? We can have cocktails in the bar!

DOROTHY: No Betty. I've got a thousand and one things to do, I'm getting married tomorrow, in case you didn't know, and I have better things to do that sit talking to you. No offence.

BETTY: Dot, when was the last time you went on a hen night.

DOROTHY: I don't believe we had them when I was young.

BETTY: Well you are not likely to go on many more, especially your own, so let's make the most of it.

DOROTHY: If you insist on taking me out, I will allow you to take me to the Royal Hotel...

BETTY: Ah!

DOROTHY: ...where I will allow you accompany me to eat from the carvery. It's very reasonable in there and you serve yourself so it is quick. That way I can be home before it gets too late to finish everything I have to do tonight.

BETTY shakes her head. TOM returns to BILL with a tray containing two pints and four large whiskeys.

TOM: I thought we had better get a few shorts in. Don't want to spend the whole night going to the toilet.

BILL: This is quite a revelation to me you know Tom. I never knew you were a drinker.

TOM: It's very rare for me Bill. Tonight is probably my last chance to let my hair down.

BILL: I didn't even know you had any.

DOROTHY puts down her tea cup.

DOROTHY: Are you coming then?

BETTY: You are in a hurry aren't you?

DOROTHY: I told you, lots to do. *(BETTY is smiling to herself.)* What's the matter with you?

BETTY: I was just thinking. You're in a hurry. Are you in a hurry to get married as well.

DOROTHY: What are you talking about?

BETTY: Is there something you haven't told me?

DOROTHY: Like what?

BETTY: I mean, a hastily arranged wedding. *Shotgun* wedding?

DOROTHY: If you're going to be stupid, you can forget about the Royal Hotel.

BETTY: OK, OK. God, it was only a joke.

DOROTHY: If that is what passes for humour in your opinion, then I would be grateful if you would remain serious.

They exit. The WAITRESS removes the tea things then appears in a coat before exiting herself. The lights on the cafe side of the stage go out. We get the impression that some time has passed in the pub. The pints are reduced and the whiskeys finished. TOM is starting to get very drunk.

TOM: Oh dear. All gone! Ha ha, better get some more eh fella?

BILL: Are you sure you're OK? Do you need a hand?

TOM: No problem old man. You stay there.

TOM picks up the empty whiskey glasses and exits. BILL takes out his mobile phone and dials. There is no answer. He puts the phone away as TOM returns with four more large whiskeys.

TOM: Ringing someone? Bored with my company?

BILL: No, no. I thought I had a text message that's all.

TOM: Did it beep?

BILL: I thought it did. Must have been mistaken.

TOM: Maybe it was a sign. You know a warning. 'Don't do it Bill'.

BILL: Very funny.

TOM: Or a reminder. You can do that can't you. Set it to beep and give you a message. 'Getting married tomorrow'.

BILL: I don't think I'm likely to forget.

TOM: Amazing things, aren't they, mobile 'phones.

BILL: Well, I suppose they have their uses.

TOM: You can be anywhere, but you can still be in touch.

BILL: I thought you didn't like them.

TOM: I'm not saying I like them. I'm just saying they have their uses that's all. It was good of her to give me one.

BILL: You mean your daughter?

TOM: Yes. Very good of her, She looks after me you know?

BILL: What does she think about Betty?

TOM: Very supportive. Says, whatever makes me happy you know?

BILL: That'snice.

TOM: It was her who got me to move up here. She said 'Dad, you have to move on. You're living in a museum'.

BILL: A museum?

TOM: I didn't like to touch anything you know?

BILL: You mean, after your wife died.

TOM: I didn't want to do anything to upset her.

BILL: Your wife?

TOM: I left everything as it was.

BILL: You mean...

TOM: She said, 'Dad, you can't go on like this'.

BILL: You mean, you didn't change anything?

TOM: She said 'You've made a shrine to Mum. But you still have your own life to lead'.

BILL: A shrine?

TOM: So she made me sell up.

BILL: You didn't want to?

TOM: She was right of course.

BILL: So you don't regret it now?

TOM: Daughter in a million she is. And lovely. Absolutely lovely.

BILL: Yes.

TOM: She would do anything for me. Anything.

BILL: You're very lucky.

TOM: Yes. Lucky. Here, keep these warm. I just need the little boys room.

TOM exits. BILL again takes out his phone and dials. This time it is answered.

BILL: Hello. Hi love, are you OK? Well, I keep meaning to come round and have a chat with you. Yes, I know it is tomorrow... Look, don't be angry, I haven't had the chance to... I know, but if... Hello. Hello?

He puts the phone away as TOM returns.

TOM: Who are you calling?

BILL: No one.

TOM: A secret lover?

BILL: Shut your face.

TOM: What? Sorry. Sorry old man, didn't mean to offend.

BILL: What were we talking about?

TOM: I have absolutely no idea.

BILL: You were telling me about your daughter.

TOM: Was I? She's lovely you know. Really lovely.

BILL: Yes you said that.

TOM: Pretty. Takes after her mother of course.

BILL: Of course.

TOM: Did I tell you she was married?

BILL: Yes. And your grandson has just been promoted.

TOM: Has he?

BILL: I believe so.

TOM: I'll tell you what. If she walked into this room now, every head would turn. She never lost it you know. Not since the day I met her.

BILL: Your daughter?

TOM: What?

BILL: You're talking about your daughter?

TOM: Don't be ridiculous. I'm not talking about my daughter. I'm talking about my wife.

BILL: Oh.

TOM: Lovely women she is.

BILL: Yes.

TOM: Such beautiful eyes. I can get lost in those eyes.

BILL: Tom...

TOM: Oh, I know. You're going to say I've had enough to drink. Well, you're probably right. Cheers. *(He drinks.)*

BILL: No, I wasn't going to say that. You obviously had a very happy marriage.

TOM: Best days of my life.

BILL: But you've moved on now.

TOM: I'm here aren't I?

BILL: Do you think Betty would have liked her?

TOM: Betty? Betty is not a patch on her.

BILL: I didn't ask that.

TOM: She's not fit to walk in her shadow.

BILL: Now, steady on.

TOM: You didn't know her. Greatest woman who ever lived my wife. What's Betty?

BILL: OK Tom. I know you've had a lot to drink. But don't insult Betty. Understand?

TOM: What?

BILL: Don't insult Betty.

TOM: Whatever you say man. Hey, don't get angry.

BILL: I'm not angry.

TOM: Good. Hey, guess who's getting married in the morning. Hey, ding dong, the bells are going to chime.

BILL: Yes.

TOM: What's the matter old man. Cold feet?

BILL: Don't be stupid.

TOM: Alright, alright. Only trying to have a good time. That's all. Just trying to have a good time.

TOM starts to get maudlin. BILL has clearly had enough of the conversation and sits staring at his drink for a while, then he gets up.

BILL: Going to the toilet.

BILL exits.

TOM: Alright old man. Alright.

Blackout

ACT 2

Scene 4

The café. The morning of the wedding. DOROTHY is sitting at the table with an empty tea cup in front of her. She is dressed for her wedding. BETTY enters.

BETTY: What the hell are you doing here? *(The WAITRESS enters.)* Go away! *(The WAITRESS exits)* Well? You are supposed to be getting married in precisely one hour.

DOROTHY: I came here to think.

BETTY: Think! What is there to think about?

DOROTHY: I can't do this Betty. I don't love him.

BETTY: And? Look, you knew that you didn't love him when you decided to get married. I knew it. You knew it. Bill knew it. I think even Tom knew it. Well maybe not. But you knew it then, and you knew that you didn't love him when we were having dinner last night. You were still going to marry him then. What's changed?

DOROTHY: I seem to have forgotten about the most important thing in my life.

BETTY: What?

DOROTHY: God.

BETTY: Oh Christ!

DOROTHY: How can I enter into the sanctity of marriage for financial reasons?

BETTY: But you do like Bill?

DOROTHY: I can't marry someone because I like them and it'll mean I can afford to get some new carpets. All my life I've loved my God. I can't do this to him now.

BETTY: Will He still know? With you getting married in a registry office?

DOROTHY: This is no time to joke. We have to find Bill and tell him.

BETTY: You haven't told him yet?

DOROTHY: There's no answer at his house and his mobile is turned off. Perhaps he stayed at Tom's. Have you got the number? I'll try there?

BETTY: Wait a moment. Let's talk about this. I understand what you say, you don't actually love Bill, but you seem to think that makes it an insult to God if you marry him.

DOROTHY: "It is a shocking and sinful way, to marry without love."

BETTY: Oh for...

DOROTHY: It's William Kirby. Le Chien D'or.

BETTY: I know, and what's more, the next line is "It's better than no way at all". There, you didn't expect me to know that did you?

DOROTHY: Betty, you astound me. Anyway, leaving aside your unexpected familiarity with nineteenth century Canadian authors...

BETTY: They made it into a mini series on TV.

DOROTHY: ... the fact is that I cannot marry Bill. I am just grateful that I came to my senses in time.

BETTY: You can't marry him. I don't suppose you've decided to shack up with him instead? *(Pause.)* No, I thought not. I've gone and bought myself a hat as well.

DOROTHY: I am grateful to you for not having the presumption that you can change my mind.

BETTY: I know you better than that.

DOROTHY: Right. Well if you could just give Tom a call I had better try to find a way to tell Bill.

TOM enters, flustered.

BETTY: Oh, Tom. Is Bill with you?

TOM: No. I've searched everywhere. I was banking on him being in here.

DOROTHY: Is he not at home?

TOM: Well, if he is he isn't answering the door. He was supposed to have come round to mine an hour ago. *(The WAITRESS enters.)* Oh, er. We had better have some tea please.

WAITRESS: He is at my house.

There is a long stunned silence.

BETTY: I'm sorry?

WAITRESS: He stayed at my house last night. He was asleep on the sofa when I came out.

BETTY: And just what the hell...

TOM: I knew that you two knew each other. I...

WAITRESS: He is my father.

DOROTHY: He's your...

BETTY: My God!

TOM: Your father?

WAITRESS: Yes.

BETTY: My God!

WAITRESS: I never knew until my Dad died. That is, my mother's husband. Then she told me. I've hardly told anyone.

BETTY: Oh my God!

DOROTHY: Will you stop saying that?

BETTY: But, Dorothy! You could have...

DOROTHY: Who is you mother er...

WAITRESS: Susan. And my mother is Ann Sharples.

BETTY: Ena?

WAITRESS: I believe some people called her that.

BETTY: Well I never. The old...

TOM: Betty! We are talking about Susan's mother here.

DOROTHY: Your father, I mean your mother's husband, never knew that you er..?

WAITRESS: Mum lied about the dates. It was easier to keep men in the dark in those days. Even Bill didn't know until recently, though I think he suspected.

TOM: Are you married Susan?

WAITRESS: Divorced. I have two boys.

BETTY: My God Dot, you could have been a step grandma!

DOROTHY: Have you got anything sensible to say? No? Then keep quiet please.

TOM: You said Bill came to yours last night?

WAITRESS: Yes. He rang me first but I wouldn't talk to him.

BETTY: I thought he was with you.

TOM: I lost him. Well, I remember him going to the toilet. I don't remember him coming back. I'd had rather a lot to drink I'm afraid.

DOROTHY: You didn't approve of the marriage?

WAITRESS: Oh I don't know. I suppose I was acting a bit spoiled. Upset that I hadn't got an invite. But we had agreed not to make it public that he was my father, so there was no way he could invite me really. I know that, but, I was just hurt, not to be part of it.

DOROTHY: So what happened when he arrived?

WAITRESS: He asked me what I thought of the marriage.

DOROTHY: And you said?

WAITRESS: He should do whatever he thought was best.

DOROTHY: He was having doubts?

WAITRESS: He had more or less decided to call it off.

BETTY: Well, of all the...

DOROTHY: Shut up Betty. Did he give a reason.

WAITRESS: Yes. He did Dorothy. He said that he wished he had met you fifty years ago. He said his life would have been very different. He said that the reason he had lived his life the way he had, was because he had never met the right woman at the right time. Now he had, and it was too late. He said you were too good for him, your reputation would be tarnished by marrying him, and you didn't deserve that.

BETTY: He said all that?

WAITRESS: I think he's had quite a bit to drink.

DOROTHY: You mean it was just the drink talking?

WAITRESS: No, I mean he was talking from the heart, without inhibition.

DOROTHY: Did he say anything else?

WAITRESS: Not really. He was going to call you but I told him to sleep on it.

BETTY: And you just left him sleeping on your sofa and came to work like nothing had happened?

WAITRESS: Well I didn't know what time the wedding was. It could have been this afternoon.

BETTY: But you didn't think to say anything to Dorothy when she walked in here?

WAITRESS: It isn't me that has something to say, it's my father. And I thought that if she has time to come in here there must be plenty of time before the wedding.

BETTY: But you must have heard us talking. You must have realised...

DOROTHY: It's alright Betty. Susan has been in a very awkward position.

BETTY: I can't believe you're being so calm about this.

DOROTHY: I'm trying to understand the situation. Last night I thought I was getting married today. This morning I have found that if I were to do so I would inherit a stepdaughter and two step grandchildren. It's all a bit of a shock and I want to keep calm to make sure I do the right thing.

BETTY: What do you mean do the right thing?

DOROTHY: I think the first thing to do is to get Bill here.

WAITRESS: I'll give him a call. *(She exits.)*

DOROTHY: Then we are going to sit down and discuss what our options are.

BETTY: You mean, do you kill him with a meat cleaver or a bread knife?

DOROTHY: I'm keeping an open mind. As I said to you earlier, I had discounted the possibility of marrying Bill because I am not prepared to enter a marriage without love.

TOM: You're not going to marry him? Oh good. Well, at least you're agreed on that.

BETTY: Wait a minute you said you *had* discounted marrying him. Past tense. Don't tell me you've changed your mind.

TOM: Well, I hope not.

BETTY: Tom, will you just keep your mouth shut?

DOROTHY: We're agreed on nothing until we actually get to speak to each other. But if he doesn't want to marry me, then it does rather make the outcome of our conversation rather obvious.

BETTY: How much did he have to drink last night?

TOM: Oh, er about four double whiskeys and a couple of pints.

BETTY: And you had the same?

TOM: Um

BETTY: Well you can cut that out for a start, if you want to carry on seeing me. I don't want a man who is a lush.

TOM: Betty, you know I seldom drink. It was his stag night remember.

BETTY: Listen to you. Stag night indeed!

TOM: And Betty. This might not be the time to say this, but I did a lot of thinking last night, after Bill had gone, and I think I might have said a few things I shouldn't have...

BETTY: Like what?

TOM: Well, I think I got a bit maudlin. Started to live in the past. The important thing is that you mean the world to me right now and I feel very lucky to have met you. I...I wish it was our wedding day.

BETTY: Are you sure you're not still drunk?

TOM: I mean it Betty.

BETTY: Thank you Tom. You mean a lot to me too.

TOM: Do you think that...

BETTY: Tom, I think we need to discuss this another time.

TOM: I understand that. *(He looks distraught.)*

BETTY: Oh Tom. For God's sake. The answer's 'yes' alright. Now, sometime, when all this is cleared up, you can get round to asking me the question.

TOM: Really?

BETTY: Really.

The WAITRESS enters.

WAITRESS: He's on his way. He was already up. He'll only be a couple of minutes.

DOROTHY: How did he sound?

WAITRESS: Relieved, I think. He said he was in a panic when he woke up, didn't know where he was, couldn't find his 'phone. He'd just about come to his senses and was about to come out looking for you when I rang.

TOM: Er, should we, er, have some tea or something?

WAITRESS: OK.

BETTY: You stay here. We'll make it. Come on you.

BETTY and TOM exit.

WAITRESS: I'm sorry. I should have said something earlier. As soon as you came in.

DOROTHY: Well, I had more or less decided to spoil my own wedding day anyway.

There is a pause whilst DOROTHY considers the WAITRESS in this new light.

DOROTHY: How did you feel when your mother told you that Bill was your father? Did you even know who he was?

WAITRESS: I had seen him a few times when I was growing up. Him and my

Dad, I can't stop calling him my Dad, actually got on quite well. Then when I left home I never really gave him another thought. When my Mum told me, I couldn't believe how the two of them could just act normal in front of my Dad. I saw my Mum in a completely new light. I hated her for a while, but I forgave her. Thank God. I mean, I made my peace with her before she died. Thank God for that.

DOROTHY: And Bill?

WAITRESS: The first time I really spoke to him was Mum's funeral. He talked about the affair. Said that it 'just sort of happened'. I didn't really want to know, but I had forgiven Mum so I couldn't really be angry with him.

DOROTHY: And do you see much of him now?

WAITRESS: No. We tried. I mean he came round for Sunday dinner a few times but we both knew that it wasn't really working. You can't suddenly start loving someone without reason can you?

DOROTHY: No. No you can't.

BILL enters. BETTY appears to see who has come in. She passes BILL to lock the cafe door to the street.

BETTY: As far as the general public is concerned, we're shut. Sit down Bill. Tea's on it's way.

BETTY exits.

BILL: Are you OK?

DOROTHY: Never felt better.

BILL: So, you know all about Susan?

DOROTHY: Yes Bill. As a matter of interest, how long were you planning to leave it before mentioning it to me that, every week, I have my tea served to me by my own stepdaughter?

BILL: Ah.

DOROTHY: You told me that you knew her mother. I didn't realise that you knew her quite so well!

BILL: Well, it was one of those things that I had to clear up but never got round to.

DOROTHY: Like this feeling that you're not good enough for me.

BILL: She, er, she told you that I'd said that?

DOROTHY: Yes, and, by the way, I'll decide what's good enough for me, thank you very much.

BILL: Listen. I can understand that you are angry.

WAITRESS: I think I had better...

DOROTHY: No, Susan. Please stay, I want you to hear this as well. Bill, I owe you an apology. I really cannot explain my behaviour. But, thank God, I woke up this morning and finally came to my senses. I don't know what has been wrong with me these last few months. I seem to have forgotten everything that is important to me. Well, this morning as I was getting ready, I finally realised what a fool I was. I put this dress on and looked at myself in the mirror and said to myself 'You idiot! What on earth do you think you are doing?' That's when I rang you, but you didn't answer; I tried your mobile and it was switched off, so I went to your house and there was no one in. So I came here. I came here and ordered a cup of tea off this poor woman, who has been serving me tea in this dreary cafe for God knows how many years, and I thought what a lying, deceitful, dishonest, untrustworthy, devious, false-hearted son of a bitch you are. All the women you have had over the years and, you know what? Every one of them better than me. Why? Because they had the common sense not to give up their lives for you. Even Betty. Poor lonely Betty, who you 'truly loved', had the wisdom to reject you in the end. You're a loser Bill. You've lost out in love and you've lost out in life. So many women, but not one true love. Shall I tell you what true love is Bill? Would you like to know? I should hate you to go to your grave having never known.

BILL: Dorothy, Look I...

DOROTHY: Love is trusting someone. Knowing that they love you. It's a reciprocal arrangement. True love lasts a life time. Whatever happens, whatever problems you have to face, you face them together, knowing that the other person is there for you. When two people love each other they remain utterly committed to each other for the whole of their lives.

BILL: Look, I understand that you are upset...

DOROTHY: Upset? I haven't even started yet Bill. You never knew my Frank, did you Bill? I was just that annoying woman who got in the way of you having your way with your boss's wife. Well, let me tell you, Frank was a giant amongst men. One in a million. When we got together people said it was a match made in heaven. Everyone said how lucky I was to have such a good man. And I knew they were right. I couldn't believe my luck. He chose me out of all the girls. How grateful I was. How lucky I was to have such a good, good man. And do you know what this good man did Bill? Do you? *He had an affair!*

WAITRESS: I really think...

DOROTHY: Stay where you are! I gave up everything for him Bill. I had a good education, I could have had a career. But no, I stayed at home and kept things nice for him, made sure he always had a clean shirt and dinner on the table when he gets home and the bastard repays me by having an affair.

WAITRESS: But, I don't think...

DOROTHY: Sit! He started coming home late, saying that there was a lot on at work. He started going away on 'business trips'. The 'phone would ring and he would take it on the extension upstairs so that he didn't 'disturb me'. He thought he was being so clever, but I could SMELL her on him. Then, suddenly, it stopped. He was a pig to me for about six months and then he went back to pretty well ignoring me, like he did before. I never told him that I knew, he probably went to his grave thinking that he had got away with it. I didn't need to tell him you see Bill. I had come to terms with it. I realised that there was no point in wasting my love on any man. It's a reciprocal arrangement Bill. It doesn't work if the love is only one way. That's when I realised that I should love only God. God and God alone. *(Pause.)* Do you know how I felt when you walked into this cafe Bill? I was pleased. You represent everything I hate about men. You use women for your own pleasure. You were like Frank a hundred times over. I already had God in my life. I had someone to love. When you walked in here I was so happy because now I had some to despise, someone to loath, someone to hate! *(She begins to screech.)* Hate Bill, Someone to Hate! Someone to HATE!

DOROTHY begins to sob. BILL indicates to the WAITRESS to move and she stands and moves a few feet away. BILL puts his hand on DOROTHY's shoulder.

BILL: But it isn't me that you hate, is it Dorothy? *(DOROTHY shakes her head.)* How many years have you carried this around with you?

DOROTHY doesn't answer but her shoulders shake as she continues to sob.

BILL: I'm sorry. He really hurt you.

DOROTHY starts to compose herself.

BILL: When I went to Susan's last night and told her that I wasn't good enough for you it was because I didn't believe you would ever love me. You've put on a great act Dorothy. You had me fooled. Seems to be a recurring theme in my life. But you don't fool me anymore. You had me believing that you had no affection for me. That our marriage was just to legitimise a financial arrangement. I went along with it because I thought that, maybe one day, you might love me. Last night I convinced myself that I could never change the way you feel about me. Now I realise that I don't need to.

DOROTHY: *(Through her sobs.)* Bill I...

BILL: I'm a simple man Dorothy. I don't know about reciprocal arrangements. But I know that I love you and that you love me.

DOROTHY: Bill...

BILL: Let me into your heart Dorothy.

DOROTHY: Are you sure?

BILL: I want this more than I've ever wanted anything in my life.

DOROTHY: I can't believe it. I...

BILL: It's OK Dorothy. There's no need for any more words. *(He kisses her. There is a pause and then they kiss again, with real affection.)* Susan, I think you had better fetch the other two.

The WAITRESS exits.

BILL: What are we like? We very nearly threw away the chance of our lifetimes.

DOROTHY: Is this really happening?

BILL: Oh yes. It's real alright.

The WAITRESS enters with BETTY and TOM.

BETTY: Well, have you two decided what you're doing?

DOROTHY: *(With great effort, the DOROTHY we know is back.)* Like you weren't stood with your ears pressed to the wall listening to everything.

BETTY: Well, I might have caught the odd word.

DOROTHY: Excellent. Well, in that case it will come as no surprise to you that Bill and I need to split up.

TOM: What?

BETTY: I thought...

DOROTHY: Well, we can't arrive at the registry office together can we? Come on.

DOROTHY beckons BETTY and the WAITRESS who both exit with her. TOM and BILL look at each other for a moment, then TOM offers BILL his hand and they have a congratulatory handshake as the curtain falls.

Curtain

Furniture and Property

Act 1

Scene 1

On Stage:

Café area: Table and four chairs.
             On table. Small vase of flowers, condiments, menu, small milk jug, sugar bowl with spoon. **Dorothy**'s tea in a cup and saucer.
             Further tables or dressings at director's discretion.

Pub area: Table and two chairs.
             Further tables or dressings at director's discretion.

Off Stage: Tray with a cup and saucer and small milk jug. (**Waitress**)

Personal: **Dorothy:** Mobile 'phone.

Act 1

Scene 2

On Stage:

Café area: Strike: Tea cups, saucers and milk jugs.

Pub area: Set: Box of dominoes.

Off Stage: Two half pint tankards of beer. (**Tom**)

87

Two half pint tankards of beer. (**Bill**)

Personal: **Tom**: Mobile 'phone.

Act 1

Scene 3

On Stage:

Café area: Strike: Tea things.
Set: **Dorothy**'s tea in a cup and saucer, small jug of milk.

Pub area: Strike: Box of Dominoes, beer tankards.
Set: **Bill**'s empty beer tankard.

Off Stage: Tray with two cups and saucers, two small milk jugs and a pot of tea. (**Waitress**)
Half pint tankard of beer. (**Tom**)
Half pint tankard of beer. (**Tom**)

Act 1

Scene 4

On Stage:

Café area: Strike: Tea things.

Pub area: Strike: Beer tankards.

Off Stage: Tray with a cup and saucer and small milk jug.
(**Waitress**)

Act 1

Scene 5

On Stage:

Café area: Reset: **Betty**'s tea in a cup and saucer, small jug of milk.

Pub area: As before.

Off Stage: Tray with a cup and saucer and small milk jug and plate of cakes on a napkin. (**Waitress**)

Act 1

Scene 6

On Stage:

Café area: Strike: Tea things and plate.
Set: **Betty**'s tea in a cup and saucer, small jug of milk.

Pub area: As before.

Off Stage: Tray with two cups and saucers, two small milk jugs and a pot of tea. (**Waitress**)
Slice of walnut cake on a plate. (**Waitress**)

Personal: **Dorothy**: Handkerchief.

Act 2

Scene 1

On Stage:

Café area:	Strike: Tea things and plate.
Pub area:	As before.
Off Stage:	Tray with four cups and saucers, four small milk jugs and a pot of tea. (**Waitress**) Fresh pot of tea. (**Waitress**)
Personal:	**Waitress:** Magazine. **Tom**: Twenty pound note.

Act 2

Scene 2

On Stage:

Café area:	Strike: Tea things.
Pub area:	Set: **Bill**'s half pint of beer.
Off Stage:	Gin and Tonic. (**Bill**)
Personal:	**Betty:** Lipstick and mirror.

Act 2

Scene 3

On Stage:

Café area:	As before.
Pub area:	Strike: Glasses.

Off Stage: Two pint tankards of beer. (**Tom**)
              Tray with two cups and saucers, two small milk jugs and a pot of tea. (**Waitress**)
              Tray with two pint tankards of beer and four large whiskies. (**Tom**)
              Four large whiskies. (**Tom**)

Personal: **Bill:** Mobile 'phone.

Act 2

Scene 4

On Stage:

Café area: Set: **Dorothy**'s tea in a cup and saucer, small jug of milk.

Pub area: Strike: Glasses and tray.

Lighting

Act 1, Scene 1

To Open: Lights come up on café.
              They exit.

              Blackout.

Act 1, Scene 2

To Open: Lights come up on pub.

> *The shuffle of the tiles commences as the lights fade.*
> Blackout.

Act 1, Scene 3

To Open: Lights come up on both areas.
DOROTHY exits.
Blackout.

Act 1, Scene 4

To Open: Lights come up on café.

Tom: ...Just wasting my time.

Blackout.

Act 1, Scene 5

To Open: Lights come up on café.
They all exit.

Blackout.

Act 1, Scene 6

To Open: Lights come up on café.

No cues.

Act 2, Scene 1

To Open: Lights come up on café.
The three follow TOM out slightly aghast at his

behaviour.

Blackout.

Act 2, Scene 2

To Open: Lights come up on pub.
BETTY: ... Aren't you getting married soon?

Blackout.

Act 2, Scene 3

To Open: Lights come up on both areas.
The WAITRESS removes the tea things then appears in a coat before exiting herself.

Fade lights on café.
TOM: Alright old man. Alright.

Blackout.

Act 2, Scene 4

To Open: Lights come up on café.

No cues.